Bulgarian Vocabulary:
A Bulgarian Language Guide

Fidanka Dourneva

Contents

Bulgarian (Български)

In 886, Bulgaria used the Glagolitic alphabet created by St. St. Cyril and Methodius. Gradually the Glagolitic alphabet was displaced by the Cyrillic alphabet created in Preslav Literary School in the beginning of X century. It contains 30 letters some of which were borrowed from the Greek alphabet and others were simplified variations of some of the Glagolitic letters.

An old variation of the Cyrillic alphabet was used in Bulgaria by the beginning of the XIX century. The transition to the Russian civil alphabet was facilitated by the noticeable presence of the Russian literature in Bulgaria. The old Cyrillic letters Ѫ and Ѭ were used in Bulgarian and missing in Russian whereas Ы and Э were not used in the Bulgarian version. The final version of the contemporary Cyrillic alphabet dates from the orthographic reform from 1945.

Many Turkish words were adopted into Bulgarian during the long period of Ottoman rule. Words have also been borrowed from Latin, Greek, Russian, French, Italian, German and increasingly from English.

Here is the contemporary variation of Bulgarian alphabet:

Bulgarian alphabet (българска азбука)

А а	Б б	В в	Г г	Д д	Е е	Ж ж	З з	И и	Й й
а	бъ	въ	гъ	дъ	е	жъ	зъ	и	и кратко
a	b	v	g	d	e	zh	z	i	y
[a/ɐ]	[b/p]	[v/f]	[g/k]	[d/t]	[ɛ]	[ʒ/ʃ]	[z/s]	[i]	[j]

К к	Л л	М м	Н н	О о	П п	Р р	С с	Т т	У у
къ	лъ	мъ	нъ	о	пъ	ръ	съ	тъ	у
k	l	m	n	o	p	r	s	t	u
[k/g]	[l/ɫ]	[m]	[n]	[ɔ/o]	[p]	[r]	[s/z]	[t/d]	[u/o]

Ф ф	Х х	Ц ц	Ч ч	Ш ш	Щ щ	Ъ ъ	ь	Ю ю	Я я
фъ	хъ	цъ	чъ	шъ	щъ	ер голям	ер малък	ю	я
f	h	ts	ch	sh	sht	a	'	yu	ya
[f]	[x]	[ts]	[tʃ]	[ʃ]	[ʃt]	[ɤ/ɐ]	[j/-]	[ju/u]	[ja/a]
								[jo/o]	[jɐ/ɐ]

Here are the Bulgarian letters with their transcription and examples:

Letter	Note	English equivalent	Sound Value	Symbol	Bulgarian word	Pronunciation	English translation
Аа	when stressed	a	arm	a	сграда	ˋzgradə	building
	when unstressed	u	sun	ə	сграда	ˋzgradə	building
Бб		b	brother	b	богат	boˋgat	rich
Вв		v	value	v	въздух	ˋvʌzduh	air
Гг		g	goat	g	гора	goˋra	forest
Дд		d	drink	d	данък	ˋdanək	tax
Ее		e	pending	e	емблема	emˋblemə	emblem
Жж		s	treasure	zh	жаба	ˋzhabə	frog
Зз		z	zebra	z	змия	zmiˋya	snake
Ии		i	pitch	i	истина	ˋistinə	truth
Йй		y	youth	y	чайка	ˋchaykə	seagull
Кк		k	karatae	k	крава	ˋkravə	cow
Лл		l	luck	l	лак	lak	polish
		l	leaf	l	любов	lyuˋbof	love
Мм		m	meat	m	минута	miˋnutə	minute
Нн		n	noble	n	нощ	nosht	night
Оо		o	pot	o	орел	oˋrel	eagle
Пп		p	pirate	p	прът	prʌt	rod
Рр		r	rodent	r	рак	rak	cancer
Сс		s	sand	s	суша	ˋsushə	drought
Тт		t	table	t	трик	trik	trick
Уу		oo	boom	u	учен	ˋuchen	scientist
Фф		f	football	f	фирма	ˋfirmə	firm

Letter	Note	English equivalent	Sound Value	Symbol	Bulgarian word	Pronunciation	English translation
Xx		h	heat	h	храна	hrə`na	food
Цц		tz	quartz	tz	цяр	tzyar	cure
Чч		ch	chimney	ch	чакал	chə`kal	jackal
Шш		sh	bluish	sh	шипка	`shipkə	Rose hip
Щщ		sht	smashed	sht	щурм	`shturm	attack
Ъъ	when stressed	u	ugly	ʌ	ъгъл	`ʌgəl	corner
	when unstressed	u	cut	ə	ъгъл	`ʌgəl	corner
ь		y	youth	y	монтьор	mon`tyor	mechanic
Юю		you	you	yu	юнак	`yunak	hero
Яя		ya	yarn	ya	ягода	`yagodə	starwberry

VOLWELS – ГЛАСНИ ЗВУКОВЕ

There are 6 vowels in Bulgarian - **а, ъ, о, у, е, и** . When a vowel is stressed it is pronounced clearly.

When unstressed, some vowels are reduced, becoming shorter and less distinct. When stressed, the letter "**ъ**" is pronounced [ʌ] and when unstressed, it's pronounced [ə]. The vowels „**е**" and „**и**" don't change their pronunciation when not stressed.

CONSONANTS – СЪГЛАСНИ ЗВУКОВЕ

There are 3 types of consonants in Bulgarian - voiced (звучни), voiceless (беззвучни) and sonorous (сонорни).

voiced	б	в	г	д	ж	з				
voiceless	п	ф	к	т	ш	с	х	ц	ч	щ
sonorous	л	м	н	р	й	ь				

There are several letters which can be represented by a combination of Latin letters. These are:

ц – tz

ч – ch

ш – sh

щ – sht

VOICED CONSONANTS - ЗВУЧНИ СЪГЛАСНИ

Every voiced consonant has a corresponding voiceless one.

voiced consonant	б	в	г	д	ж	з
corresponding voiceless consonant	п	ф	к	т	ш	с

Voiced consonants are reduced to their corresponding voiceless one when:

   a) at the end of a word – (e.g. хля**б** - bread) is pronounced like - хля**п** [hlyap] (“**б**” becomes “**п**”)

b) immediately before any voiceless consonant – (e.g. общ - general) is pronounced like опщ [opsht] (again, "**б**" becomes "**п**")

This is very common in Bulgarian language. Here are some more examples with the rest of the voiced consonants.

в – ф - моли**в** (pencil) – моли**ф** [`molif]

г – к - ми**г** (instant, moment) - ми**к** [mik]

д – т - ло**д**ка (boat) - ло**т**ка [`lotkə]

ж – ш - беле**ж**ка (note) - беле**ш**ка [be`leshkə]

з – с - изра**з** (expresion) - изра**с** [`izrəs]

VOICELESS CONSONANTS - БЕЗЗВУЧНИ СЪГЛАСНИ

Most voiceless consonants have corresponding voiced ones. Those which don't have a corresponding voiced consonant don't change their pronunciation.

voiceless consonant	п	ф	к	т	ш	с	х	ц	ч	щ
corresponding voiced consonant	б	в	г	д	ж	з	-	-	-	-

A voiceless consonant is pronounced like its corresponding voiced one when

a) before a voiced consonant – (e.g. **с**града – building) should be pronounced like **з**града [`zgradə]. Since "**г**" is a voiced consonant, "**с**" to become "**з**".

More examples:

т - д – сватба (wedding) - свадба [`svadbə], отгатвам (guess) - одгатвам [od`gatvəm]

с- з – сборник (collection, book) - зборник [`zbornik], сган (mob) – зган [zgan],

SONOROUS CONSONANTS - СОНОРНИ СЪГЛАСНИ

The third type of consonants are called sonorous. They are **л, м, р, н, й** and **ь**. They can be easily memorized with the word **ламарина** [ləmə`rinə] (meaning laminated iron) which contains most of them except for **й** and **ь**.

The sonorous letter "**л**" changes its pronunciation depending on its position. It is pronounced softly before **е, и, ю** and **я** (like in the words "love", "leaf" or "like"). It is pronounced by touching the tongue to the teeth before **а, ъ, о, у** and a consonant as well as at the end of the word (like in "last", large", etc.)

The letter "**й**" looks like the vowel "**и**" but is actually a consonant. Its name in Bulgarian means "a short **и**". It is pronounced like the vowel" **и**" but shorter. It stands before "**о**" or after a vowel – район [rə`yon], герой ([ge`roy] – hero, йо-йо ([`yoyo], etc.

The letter **ь** (ер малък) doesn't have its own sound. Its purpose is to make a consonant sound softer. It is used only in combination with **о – ьо** (yo). The combination **ьо** has the same pronunciation as **йо** (yo). The difference between the two is that "**йо**" is used in the beginning of the word and after a vowel – **Йордан** [Yor`dan] – male name, майор [ma`yor] –

major and **ьо** is only used after a consonant – монтьор [mon`tyor] – mechanic, Кольо [`Kolyo] - male name, etc.

COMPOUND SOUNDS – СЪСТАВНИ ЗВУЦИ

The letters **ю** and **я** represent compound sounds. They are both combination of a consonant and a vowel.

> **ю=й+у** (yu)
>
> **я=й+а** (ya or yə) or **й+ъ** (yʌ or yə)

The digraphs дж [dzh], дз [dz] and пш [psh] are not considered separate letters.

THE STRESS - УДАРЕНИЕТО

The stress is very important for the pronunciation, as well as for the meaning of the word. There are no rules for the position of the stress in Bulgarian so every word should be memorized separately. Sometimes, the stress changes its position when changing the form (e.g. from singular to plural or when adding a definite article). Here are some examples:

нещо [`neshto] – a thing vs. неща [ne`shta] - thing**s**

песен [`pesen] - a song vs. песента [pesen`ta] - **the** song

There are words which change their meaning depending on the stress. These are the only words in Bulgarian which have written stress! For example:

вълна [`vʌlnə] – wool vs. вълнá [vəl`na] - wave

зáвет [`zavet] – lee, shelter vs. завéт [zə`vet] - legacy

рóден [`roden] – native vs. родéн [ro`den] – born

1) Measurements

weight
težina
тежина

---

area
площ
`plosh

---

case
кутия
ku`tiy

---

centimeter
сантиметър
səntim`etə

---

cup
чаша
`chash

---

dash
щипка
`shtipk

---

degree
градус
`gradu

---

depth
дълбочина
dəlbochi`n

digit
единица
edi`nitz

dozen
дузина
du`zin

foot
фут
fu

gallon
галон
gəl`o

gram
грам
gra

height
височина
visochi`n

huge
огромен
ogro`me

inch

инч

inc

kilometer

километър

kilo`metə

length

дължина

dəlzhi`n

liter

литър

`litə

little

малко

`malk

measure

мярка

`myark

meter

метър

`metə

mile

миля

`mily

minute

минута

mi`nut

miniature

миниатюрен

minia`tyure

ounce

унция

`untziy

perimeter

периметър

peri`metə

pint

пинта

`pint

pound

паунд

`paun

quart

кварта

`kvart

ruler

линия

`liniy

scale

скала

skə`l

---

small

малък

`malə

Tablespoon

супена лъжица

`supenə lə`zhitzə

Teaspoon

чаена лъжица

`chaenə lə`zhitzə

---

ton

тон

`to

---

unit

единица

edi`nitz

---

volume

обем

o`be

---

weigh

тежа

te`zh

---

weight
тегло
te`gl

width
широчина
shirochi`n

yard
ярд
`yar

Time

What time is it?
Колко е часът?
`kolko e chə`sə

It's 1:00 AM/PM
1:00 ч. сутринта/следобед е.
sutrin`ta/sled`obed

It's 2:00 AM/PM
2:00 ч. сутринта/следобед е.
sutrin`ta/sled`obed

It's 3:00 AM/PM
3:00 ч. сутринта/следобед е.
sutrin`ta/sled`obed

It's 4:00 AM/PM

4:00 ч. сутринта/следобед е.

sutrin`ta/sled`obed

It's 5:00 AM/PM

5:00 ч. сутринта/следобед е.

sutrin`ta/sled`obed

It's 6:00 AM/PM

6:00 ч. сутринта/следобед е.

sutrin`ta/sled`obed

It's 7:00 AM/PM

7:00 ч. сутринта/следобед е.

sutrin`ta/sled`obed

It's 8:00 AM/PM

8:00 ч. сутринта/следобед е.

sutrin`ta/sled`obed

It's 9:00 AM/PM

9:00 ч. сутринта/следобед е.

sutrin`ta/sled`obed

It's 10:00 AM/PM

10:00 ч. сутринта/следобед е.

sutrin`ta/sled`obed

It's 11:00 AM/PM

11:00 ч. сутринта/следобед е.

sutrin`ta/sled`obed

It's 12:00 AM/PM

12:00 ч. сутринта/следобед е.

sutrin`ta/sled`obed

---

in the morning

сутринта

sutrin`t

---

in the afternoon

следобед

sled`obe

---

in the evening

вечерта

vecher`t

---

at night

през нощта

prez nosh`t

---

afternoon

следобед

sled`obe

---

annual

годишен

go`dishe

---

calendar

календар

kəlen`da

---

daytime

през деня

prez de`ny

decade

десетилетие

deseti`leti

evening

вечер

`veche

hour

час

cha

midnight

полунощ

polu`nosh

minute

минута

mi`nut

morning

сутрин

`sutri

month

месец

`meset

night

нощ

nosh

---

nighttime

през нощта

prez nosht`t

---

noon

обед

`obe

---

now

сега

se`g

---

o'clock

часа

chə`s

---

past

минало

`minəl

---

present

настояще

nasto`yasht

---

second

секунда

se`kund

---

sunrise

изгрев

`izgre*

sunset

залез

`zale*

today

днес

dne

tonight

довечера

do`vecher

tomorrow

утре

utr

watch

часовник

chə`sovni

week

седмица

`sedmitz*

year

година

go`din

yesterday

вчера

`vcher

Months of the Year

January

януари

yanu`ar

February

февруари

fevru`ar

March

март

mar

April

април

әp`ri

May

май

ma

June

юни

`yun

July
юли
`yul

August
август
`avgus

September
септември
sep`temvr

October
октомври
ok`tomvr

November
ноември
no`emvr

December
декември
de`kemvr

Days of the Week

Monday
понеделник
pone`delni

Tuesday

вторник

`ftorni

Wednesday

сряда

`sryad

Thursday

четвъртък

chet`vərtə

Friday

петък

`petə

Saturday

събота

`səbot

Sunday

неделя

ne`dely

Seasons

winter

зима

`zim

---

spring

пролет

`prole

---

summer

лято

`lyat

---

fall/autumn

есен

`ese

Numbers

One (1)

едно

ed`n

Two (2)

две

dv

Three (3)

три

tr

Four (4)

четири

`chetir

Five (5)

пет

pe

Six (6)

шест

shes

Seven (7)

седем

`sede

Eight (8)

осем

`ose

Nine (9)

девет

`deve

Ten (10)

десет

`dese

Eleven (11)

единайсет

edi`nayse

Twelve (12)

дванайсет

dva`nayse

Twenty (20)

двайсет

`dvayse

Fifty (50)

петдесет

petde`se

Hundred (100)

сто

st

Thousand (1000)

хиляда

hi`lyad

Ten Thousand (10,000)

десет хиляди

`deset `hilyəd

One Hundred Thousand (100,000)

сто хиляди

sto `hilyəd

Million (1,000,000)

милион

mili`o

Billion (1,000,000,000)

милиард

mili`ar

Ordinal Numbers

first

първи

`pərv

---

second

втори

`ftor

---

third

трети

`tret

---

fourth

четвърти

chet`vərt

---

fifth

пети

`pet

---

sixth

шести

`shest

---

seventh

седми

`sedm

---

eighth

осми

`osm

---

ninth

девети

de`vet

---

tenth

десети

de`set

---

eleventh

единайсети

edi`nayset

---

twelfth

дванайсети

dvə`nayset

---

thirteenth

тринайсети

tri`nayset

---

twentieth

двайсети

`dvayest

---

twenty-first

двадесет и първи

`dvayest i `pərv

---

hundredth

стотен

`stote`

---

thousandth

хиляден

`hilyəde`

---

millionth

милионен

`mili`one`

---

billionth

милиарден

`mili`arde`

Geometric Shapes

angle

ъгъл

`əgə`

---

circle

кръг

`krə`

---

cone

конус

`konu`

cube
куб
ku

cylinder
цилиндър
tzi`lində

heart
сърце
sər`tz

heptagon
седмоъгълник
sedmo`əgəlni

hexagon
шестоъгълник
shesto`əgəlni

line
линия
`liniy

octagon
осмоъгълник
osmo`əgəlni

oval
елипса
`elips

parallel lines

успоредни линии

`usporedni `lini

pentagon

петоъгълник

peto`əgəlni

perpendicular lines

перпендикулярни линии

perpendiku`lyarni `lini

polygon

многоъгълник

mnogo`əgəlni

pyramid

пирамида

pirə`mid

rectangle

правоъгълник

prəvo`əgəlni

rhombus

ромб

rom

square

квадрат

kvəd`ra

star

звезда

zvez`d

---

trapezoid

трапец

trə`pet

---

triangle

триъгълник

tri`əgəlni

---

vortex

вихър

vi`hə

Colors

beige

бежов

`bezho

---

black

черен

`chere

---

blue

син

si

---

brown

кафяв

kə`fya

fuchsia

цикламен

tzi`klame

gray

сив

si

green

зелен

ze`le

indigo

индиго

in`dig

maroon

кестеняв

keste`nya

navy blue

тъмносин

`təmosi

orange

оранжев

o`ranzhe

pink

розов

`rozo

purple

лилав

əp`ri

red

червен

li`la

silver

сребърен

`srebəre

tan

светлокафяв

`svetlokəfya

teal

синьо-зелен

`sinyo-zele

turquoise

тюркоазен

tyurko`aze

violet

морав

`morə

white

бял

bya

---

yellow

жълт

zhəl

Related Verbs

to add

добавям

do`bavyə

---

to change

променям

pro`menyə

---

to check

проверявам

prove`ryavə

---

to color

оцветявам

otzve`tyavə

---

to count

броя

bro`y

---

to divide
разделям
raz`delyə

to figure
изчислявам
izchis`lyavə

to fill
попълвам
po`pəlvə

to guess
предполагам
pedpo`lagə

to measure
измервам
iz`mervə

to multiply
умножавам
umno`zhavə

to subtract
изваждам
iz`vazhdə

to take
взимам
`vzemə

to tell time

казвам часа

`kazvəm chə`s

---

to verify

потвърждавам

potvyrzh`davə

---

to watch

гледам

`gledə

Michael is a **ten** year old boy who lives in Georgia. His family owns a **twenty acre** farm; he has **two** brothers and **three** sisters. Michael loves to work on his family's farm. He and his brothers wake up at **6:00 in the morning** every day. His favorite thing to do is ride his **brown** and **white** horse around the **perimeter** of the farm to check the fencing for damage. Even if there is only a **centimeter** of damaged wood, Michael must repair it. He also has to **measure** the **height** and **width** of the fence. He takes this job very seriously, so he doesn't want to miss a thing. Michael especially loves working on the farm in **autumn** because they sell more than **one thousand orange** pumpkins during the **month** of **October!** People from all over the state travel for **miles** to buy their pumpkins. Some of their pumpkins **weigh** as much as **one hundred pounds!** In the **winter**, his family sells Christmas trees. He loves helping other families find the perfect tree, whether it is **four feet, seven feet**, or even **nine feet tall**! In **December**, his family sells a **dozen green** trees a **day**, this keeps Michael very busy. In the **spring**, his family prepares the crops for the **summer** and **autumn** harvest. Because **spring** is such a busy **time** in school, each of the siblings take turns with special projects on the farm during the **week**; Michael's is the **first** day of the week, **Monday;** Henry's is the **second** day, **Tuesday;** Alan's is the **third** day, **Wednesday**; Sally's is the **fourth** day, **Thursday;** and Ann's is the **fifth** day, **Friday**. Little Ella is still too young for chores, but she loves to **measure** the **height** of the blooming **red** and **yellow** flowers with her **small ruler**. She is a **miniature** version of their mom. She cannot wait to grow up and help around the farm. During **summer**, Michael spends most of his **time** helping his mom cook. It is so hot outside, especially in **July** and **August**; he decided he needed a fun indoor activity. While cooking, he is learning how to convert different types of **measures**, like how many **teaspoons** are in a **tablespoon** and how many **cups** are in a **gallon**; he is also learning to add a **dash** here and **sprinkle** a **little** there to make the recipe just right. Mom knows cooking is a good skill to learn, but she also knows he will be learning these **measurements** in school this **September**.

Майкъл е момче на **десет** години, което живее в Джорджия. Семейството му притежава ферма от **двайсет акра**. Той има **двама** братя и **три** сестри. Майкъл много обича да работи във фермата на своите родители. Той и братята му стават в **6:00 ч. сутринта** всеки ден. Любимото му нещо е да язди своя кон в **кафяво** и **бяло** в **периметъра** на фермата, за да проверява оградата за повреди. Дори да има и **сантиметър** повредено дърво, Майкъл трябва да го поправи. Той трябва да **измери** и **височината** и **широчината** на оградата. Той приема работата си много сериозно, затова не иска да пропусне нищо. Майкъл особено много обича да работи във фермата през **есента**, защото продават повече от **хиляда оранжеви** тикви през

месец октомври! Хората от цялата страна изминават **мили**, за да купят техните тикви. Някои от техните тикви **тежат сто паунда**! През **зимата** семейството му продава коледни елхи. Той обича да помага на други семейства да открият перфектното дърво, независимо дали то ще е **високо четири фута**, **седем фута** или дори **девет фута**! През **декември** семейството му продава **дузина зелени** дървета на **ден,** което прави Майкъл много зает. През пролетта семейството му подготвя културите за **лятно** и **есенно** прибиране на реколтата. Тъй като **пролетта** е толкова натоварено **време** в училище, всичките братя и сестри се редуват със специални проекти във фермата през **седмицата. Понеделник, първият** ден от седмицата е на Майкъл; **вторник, вторият** ден е на Хенри; **сряда, третият** ден е на Алан; **четвъртък, четвъртият** ден е на Сали, а **петък, петият** ден е на Ан. Ела все още е прекалено малка за домакинска работа, но тя обожава да **мери височината** на цъфналите **червени** и **жълти** цветя с **малката** си **линия**. Тя е **миниатюрна** версия на майка им. Тя няма търпение да порасне и да помага във фермата. През **лятото** Майкъл прекарва повечето **време** да помага на майка си в готвенето. Толкова е горещо навън, особено през **юли** и **август**; той решава, че се нуждае от забавно занимание на закрито. Докато готви, той се учи да превръща различни видове **мерки**, като например колко **чаени лъжички** правят една **супена лъжица** и колко **чаши** има в един **галон**. Той се учи и как да добави **малко** тук и да **поръси малко** там, за да направи рецептата отлична. Мама знае, че готвенето е умение, което е добре да се научи, но тя знае и, че той ще учи тези **мерки** в училище през **септември**.

2) Weather

air
въздух
`vəzdu

air pollution
замърсяване на въздуха
zamər`syavəne na `vəzduh

atmosphere
атмосфера
ətmo`sfer

avalanche
лавина
lə`vin

barometer
барометър
baro`metə

barometric pressure
атмосферно налягане
ətmo`sferno na`lyagən

blizzard
виелица
vi`elitz

breeze

бриз

bri

---

climate

климат

`klimə

---

cloud

облак

`oblə

---

cold

студен

stu`de

---

cold front

студен фронт

stu`den fron

---

condensation

кондензация

konden`zaciy

---

cool

хладно

`hladn

---

cyclone

циклон

tzi`klo

---

degree

градус

`gradu

---

depression

падина

pədi`n

---

dew

роса

ro`s

---

dew point

точка на оросяване

`tochkə na oro`syavən

---

downpour

порой

po`ro

---

drift

течение

te`cheni

---

drizzle

ситен дъжд

`siten dəzh

---

drought

суша

`sush

---

dry

сух

su

dust devil

пясъчен дявол

`pyasəchen `dyavo

duststorm

пясъчна буря

[`pyasəchna `bury

easterly wind

източен вятър

`iztochen `vyatə

evaporation

изпаряване

izpə`ryavən

eye of the storm

окото на бурята

o`koto na `buryat

fair

ясен

`yase

fall

валеж

va`lez

flash flood

порой

po`ro

flood

наводнение

navod`neni

flood stage

ниво на наводнение

ni`vo nə nəvod`neni

flurries (snow)

кратки превалявания

`kratki prevə`lyavəniy

fog

мъгла

məg`l

forecast

прогноза

prog`noz

freeze

замръзвам

zam`rʌzvə

freezing rain

замръзнал дъжд

zam`rʌznəl dʌzh

front (cold/hot)

фронт (студен/топъл)

[front (stuˈden/ˈtopəl)]

---

frost

скреж

skrez

---

funnel cloud

фуниевиден облак

funieˈviden ˈoblə

---

global warming

глобално затопляне

gloˈbalno zəˈtoplyən

---

gust of wind

порив на вятър

ˈporif na ˈvyatə

---

hail

градушка

grəˈdushk

---

haze

мараня

mərəˈny

---

heat

жега

ˈzheg

---

heat index

топлинен индекс

top`linen `indek

---

heat wave

гореща вълна

go`reshtə vəl`n

---

high

висок

vi`so

---

humid

влажен

`vlazhe

---

humidity

влажност

`vlazhnos

---

hurricane

ураган

urə`ga

---

ice

лед

le

---

ice crystals

ледени кристали

`ledeni kris`tal

---

ice storm

снежна буря

`snezhnə `bury

icicle

висулка

vi`sulk

jet stream

реактивна струя

reak`tivnə `struy

landfall

срутване на почвата

`srutvəne nə `pochvət

lightning

светкавица

svet`kavitz

low

нисък

`nisə

low pressure system

система за ниско налягане

sis`temə za `nisko nə`lyagən

meteorologist

метеоролог

meteoro`lo

meteorology

метеорология

meteoro`logiy

---

microburst

миниторнадо

`minitor`nad

---

mist

мъгла

mə`gl

---

moisture

влага

`vlag

---

monsoon

мусон

mu`so

---

muggy

задушен

za`dushe

---

nor'easter

североизточен вятър

severo`iztochen `vyatə

---

normal

нормален

nor`male

---

outlook

изглед

`izgle

---

overcast

облачен

`oblǝche

---

ozone

озон

oz`o

---

partly cloudy

разкъсана облачност

rǝz`kǝsǝnǝ `oblǝchnos

---

polar

полярен

po`lyare

---

pollutant

замърсител

zamǝr`site

---

precipitation

валеж

vǝ`lez

---

pressure

налягане

nǝ`lyagǝn

---

radar

радар

rə`da

---

radiation

радиация

rədi`atziy

---

rain

дъжд

dəzh

---

rainbow

дъга

də`g

---

rain gauge

дъждомер

dəzhdo`me

---

relative humidity

относителна влажност

otno`sitelnə `vlazhnos

---

sandstorm

пясъчна буря

`pyasəchnə `bury

---

season

сезон

se`zo

---

shower

валеж

və`lez

---

sky

небе

ne`b

---

sleet

суграшица

sug`rashitz

---

slush

киша

`kish

---

smog

смог

smo

---

smoke

пушек

`pushe

---

snow

сняг

snya

---

snowfall

снеговалеж

snegovə`lez

---

snowflake

снежинка

sne`zhink

---

snow flurry

снежна вихрушка

`snezhnə vih`rushk

---

snow shower

снеговалеж

snegovə`lez

---

snowstorm

снежна буря

`snezhnə `bury

---

spring

пролет

`prole

---

storm

буря

`bury

---

storm surge

щормова вълна

`stormovə vəln

---

stratosphere

стратосфера

strato`sfer

---

summer

лято

`lyat

---

sunrise

изгрев

`izgre

---

sunset

залез

`zale

---

supercell

суперклетка

`super`kletk

---

surge

голяма вълна

go`lyamə vəl`n

---

swell

издатина

izdəti`n

---

temperature

температура

temperə`tur

---

thaw

размразяване

rəzmrə`zyavən

---

thermal
топлинен
top`line

---

thermometer
термометър
termo`metə

---

thunder
гръм
grʌ

---

thunderstorm
гръмотевична буря
grəmo`tevichnə `bury

---

tornado
торнадо
tor`nad

---

trace
следа
sle`d

---

tropical
тропически
tro`picheski

---

tropical depression
тропическа депресия
tro`picheskə dep`resiy

---

tropical storm

тропическа буря

tro`picheskə `bury

---

turbulence

турбулентност

turbu`lentnos

---

twister

торнадо

tor`nad

---

typhoon

тайфун

təy`fu

---

unstable

нестабилен

nestə`bile

---

visibility

видимост

`vidimos

---

vortex

вихрушка

vih`rushk

---

warm

топъл

`topə

---

warning

предупреждение

preduprezh`deni

---

watch

сигнал

sig`na

---

weather

време

`vrem

---

weather pattern

метеорологичен модел

meteorolo`gichen mo`del

---

weather report

прогноза за времето

prog`nozə zə `vremet

---

weather satellite

метеорологичен сателит

meteorolo`gichen səte`li

---

westerly wind

западен вятър

`zapəden `vyatə

---

whirlwind

вихрушка

vih`rushk

---

wind

вятър

`vyatə

---

wind chill

охлаждащ вятър

oh`lazhdəsht `vyatə

---

winter

зима

`zim

Related Verbs

to blow

духам

`duhə

---

to clear up

изяснявам се

izyəs`nyavəm s

---

to cool down

изстивам

izs`tivə

---

to drizzle

ръми

rə`m

to feel
чувствам
`chuvstvə

to forecast
предсказвам
pred`skazvə

to hail
вали град
və`li gra

to rain
вали дъжд
və`li dyzh

to report
докладвам
dok`ladvə

to shine
грея
`grey

to snow
вали сняг
və`li snya

to storm
има буря
`imə `bury

to warm up

затоплям

za`toplyə

---

to watch

гледам

`gledə

Heather loves the **seasons** and **weather**. She dreams of one day becoming a **meteorologist** so she can share her love with everyone. She is currently attending school to study the **weather** and how it works. She is learning that each of the four **seasons** brings its own **weather patterns** to the world. She is amazed at how the **seasons** affect the **weather**. The **seasons** vary throughout the world, but here in America, where Heather lives, there are four distinct **seasons**, and each of them brings something different to our world. In **winter**, the **temperature** is **cold** and the ground is white with **snow**. The **wind** gets so **cold** up on the mountaintop that the **wind chill** is below zero **degrees**. Sometimes, the **wind** blows with such force that it causes an **avalanche** of **snow** on the mountain. When the **air** is this **cold**, you are likely to wake up with **frost** on your car. In the **spring**, things begin to **heat** up. The **temperature** begins to **warm** up a bit, making the **snow** on the ground **thaw** out. The flowers begin to bloom and the trees begin to grow leaves. **Spring** often brings **rain**; sometimes the **rain** is so heavy, it causes **flash floods**. A common sighting in spring is a beautiful **rainbow** after the **rain**. The **temperature** is **hot** in the **summer**. The **temperatures** begin to rise and the **heat index** goes up causing a **heat wave**. There is not much **precipitation** in **summer**; however, occasionally the **clouds** bring a **thunderstorm**. The **rain** usually does not last long in

summer, but the **thunder** and **lightning** can be dangerous. Every time there is a **thunderstorm**, Heather will watch the **weather report** to see if they will issue a **watch** or a **warning**. After **summer**, **fall** brings the start of **cool temperatures**. The leaves on the trees begin to fall, preparing the tree for the **winter**. In the coastal regions, **hurricanes** become a problem in the **fall**. This is a dangerous, yet exciting time in the world of **meteorology**. The **seasons** have a huge effect on **weather**; however the biggest changes in **weather** and the most dangerous events, such as **tsunamis**, **tornados**, and **storms**, occur during the change in **seasons**. The **unstable** and ever-changing **temperatures** affect the **barometric pressure** in a way that causes these types of events. While dangerous, they are exciting to someone like Heather who studies the **weather**. Heather's goal is to one day help educate and warn people in advance when these events are likely to occur.

Хедър обожава **сезоните** и **времето**. Тя мечтае един ден да стане **метеоролог,** за да може да сподели любовта си с всички. В момента тя ходи в училище, където изучава **времето** и как работи то. Тя учи, че всичките четири **сезона** дават своите **метеорологични модели** на света. Тя е изумена от това как **сезоните** влияят на **времето**. **Сезоните** са различни по света, но тук в Америка, където живее Хедър, има четири отделни **сезона** и всеки от тях дава нещо различно на света ни. През **зимата температурата** е **студена** и земята е побеляла от **сняг**. **Вятърът** става толкова **студен** на върха на планината, че **охлаждането от вятъра** е под нула **градуса**. Понякога **вятърът** духа с такава сила, че предизвиква **лавина** от **сняг** в планината. Когато **въздухът** е толкова **студен**, обикновено се събуждате със **скреж** на колата. През

пролетта нещата започват да се **затоплят**. **Температурата** започва да се **затопля**, което кара снега по земята да се **размразява**. Цветята започват да цъфтят и по дърветата започват да растат листа. **Пролетта** често носи **дъжд;** понякога **дъждът** е толкова силен, че причинява **порои**. Често явление през пролетта е красива **дъга** след **дъжда**. **Температурата** е **гореща** през **лятото**. **Температурите** започват да се покачват и **топлинният индекс** се покачва, причинявайки **гореща вълна**. Няма много **валежи** през **лятото**, но понякога **облаците** носят **гръмотевични бури**. **Дъждът** обикновено не продължава дълго през **лятото**, но **гръмотевиците** и **светкавиците** могат да бъдат опасни. Всеки път, когато има **гръмотевична буря,** Хедър гледа **прогнозата за времето,** за да види дали ще подадат **сигнал** или **предупреждение**. След **лятото есента** поставя началото на **студените температури**. Листата на дърветата започват да падат, подготвяйки дървото за **зимата**. В крайбрежните региони **ураганите** стават проблем през **есента.** Това е опасно, но вълнуващо време в света на **метеорологията. Сезоните** имат огромно влияние върху **времето**. Най-големите промени във **времето** обаче и най-опасните събития, като **цунами, торнадо** и **бури,** се случват при смяна на **сезоните. Нестабилните** и вечно променящи се **температури** влияят на **атмосферното налягане** по начин, който причинява този вид събития. Макар и опасни, те са вълнуващи за някой като Хедър, който изучава **времето**. Целта на Хедър е един ден да помогне за това хората да се образоват и да се предупреждават предварително, когато тези събития могат да се случат.

3) People

athlete
атлет
ət`le

---

baby
бебе
`beb

---

boy
момче
mom`ch

---

boyfriend
приятел
pri`yate

---

brother
брат
bra

---

brother-in-law
девер/шурей/баджанак
`dever/`shurey/bədzhə`na

---

businessman
бизнесмен
`biznesme

---

candidate

кандидат

kəndi`da

---

child/children

дете/ деца

de`te/de`tz

---

coach

треньор

tre`nyo

---

cousin

братовчед

brətov`che

---

customer

клиент

kli`en

---

daughter

дъщеря

dəshte`ry

---

daughter-in-law

снаха

snə`h

---

driver

шофьор

sho`fyo

---

family
семейство
se`meystv

farmer
фермер
`ferme

father/dad
баща/татко
bə`shta/`tatk

father-in-law
свекър/тъст
`svekər/tʌs

female
женски
`zhensk

friend
приятел
priya`te

girl
момиче
mo`mich

girlfriend
приятелка
pri`yatelk

godparents

кръстници

`krəstnitz`

grandchildren

внуци

`vnutz`

granddaughter

внучка

`vnuchk`

grandfather

дядо

`dyad`

grandmother

баба

`bab`

grandparents

баба и дядо

`babə i `dyad`

grandson

внук

`vnu`

husband

съпруг

`səp`ru`

instructor

инструктор

ins`trukto

---

kid

дете

de`t

---

king

крал

kra

---

male

мъжки

`mʌzhk

---

man

мъж

mʌz

---

mother/mom

майка/мама

`maykə/`mam

---

mother-in-law

свекърва/тъща

sve`kʌrvə/`tʌsht

---

nephew

племенник

`plemenni

---

niece

племенница

`plemennitz

---

parent

родител

ro`dite

---

people

хора

`hor

---

princess

принцеса

prin`tzes

---

queen

кралица

krə`litz

---

rock star

рок звезда

rok zvez`d

---

sister

сестра

ses`tr

---

sister-in-law

зълва/етърва

`zʌvə/e`tʌrv

---

son
син
si

son-in-law
зет
ze

student
ученик
uche`ni

teenager
тийнейджър
tiy`neydzhə

tourist
турист
tu`ris

wife
съпруга
səp`rug

woman
жена
zhe`n

youth
младеж
mlə`dez

Characteristics

attractive

привлекателен

privle`katele

---

bald

плешив

ple`shi

---

beard

брада

brə`d

---

beautiful

красив

krə`si

---

black hair

черна коса

`chernə ko`s

---

blind

сляп

slya

---

blond

рус

ru

---

blue eyes

сини очи

`sini o`ch

brown eyes

кафяви очи

kə`fyavi o`ch

brown hair

кестенява коса

keste`nyavə ko`s

brunette

брюнетка

bryu`netkə

curly hair

къдрава коса

`kədrəva ko`s

dark

тъмен

`təme

deaf

глух

glu

divorced

разведен

rəz`vede

elderly

възрастен

`vʌzrəste

fair (skin)

светла (кожа)

`svetlə (ko`sa

fat

дебел

de`be

gray hair

сива коса

`sivə ko`s

green eyes

зелени очи

ze`leni o`ch

handsome

красив

krə`si

hazel eyes

пъстри очи

`pəstri o`ch

heavyset

набит

nə`bi

light brown

светлокафяв

`svetlokə`fya

---

long hair

дълга коса

`dəlgə ko`s

---

married

женен/омъжена

`zhenen / o`mʌzhen

---

mustache

мустаци

mus`tatz

---

old

стар

sta

---

olive

мургав

`murgə

---

overweight

с наднормено тегло

s nəd`normeno teg`l

---

pale

блед

ble

---

petite
дребничък
`drebnichə

plump
закръглен
zək`rʌgle

pregnant
бременна
`bremenn

red head
червена коса
cher`venə ko`s

short
нисък
`nisə

short hair
къса коса
`kəsa ko`s

skinny
много слаб
`mnogo sla

slim
слаб
sla

stocky

як

ya

---

straight hair

права коса

`pravə ko`s

---

tall

висок

vi`so

---

tanned

загорял

zago`rya

---

thin

слаб

sla

---

wavy hair

чуплива коса

chup`livə ko`s

---

well built

добре сложен

dob`re `slozhe

---

white

бял

bya

---

young

млад

mla

Stages of Life

adolescence

юношество

`yunoshestv

adult

възрастен

`vəzrəste

anniversary

годишнина

go`dishnin

birth

раждане

`razhdən

death

смърт

smʌr

divorce

развод

rəz`vo

elderly

възрастни

`vʌzrəstn

---

graduation

дипломиране

diplo`mirən

---

infant

бебе

`beb

---

marriage

брак

bra

---

middle aged

на средна възраст

nə `srednə `vʌzrəs

---

newborn

новородено

novoro`den

---

preschooler

в предучилищна възраст

v `preduchilishtnə `vʌzrəs

---

preteen

предпубертетен

predpuber`tete

---

senior citizen

възрастен гражданин

`vʌzrasten `grazhdəni

---

teenager

тийнейджър

tiy`neydzhə

---

toddler

дете, което прохожда

de`te ko`eto pro`hozhd

---

tween

дете на 11 или 12 години

de`te na 11 ili 12 go`din

---

young adult

млад човек

mlat cho`ve

---

youth

младеж

mlə`des

Religion

Atheist/Agnostic

атеист/агностик

ate`ist/agnos`ti

Baha'i

бахайски

bə`haysk

Buddhist

будист

bu`dis

Christian

християнин

hristi`yani

Hindu

индус

`indu

Jewish

евреин

ev`rei

Muslim

мюсюлманин

myusyul`mani

Sikh

сикх

sik

Work

accountant

счетоводител

schetovo`dite

actor

актьор

ək`tyo

associate

сътрудник

sət`rudni

astronaut

астронавт

əstro`nav

banker

банкер

bən`ke

butcher

бакалин

bə`kali

carpenter

дърводелец

dərvo`delet

chef

главен готвач

`glaven got`vac*

clerk

чиновник

chi`novni

composer

композитор

kompo`zito

custodian

попечител

pope`chite

dentist

зъболекар

zəbo`lekə

doctor

лекар

`lekə

electrician

електротехник

elektroteh`ni

executive

администратор

ədminis`trato

farmer

фермер

`ferme`

fireman

пожарникар

pozhərni`ka

handyman

момче за всичко

mom`che zə `vsichk

judge

съдия

sədi`y

landscaper

озеленител

ozele`nite

lawyer

адвокат

ədvo`ka

librarian

библиотекар

bibliote`ka

manager

мениджър

`menidzə

model

модел

mo`de

notary

нотариус

no`tariu

nurse

медицинска сестра

medi`tzinskə ses`tr

optician

оптик

op`ti

pharmacist

фармацевт

fərmə`tzev

pilot

пилот

pi`lo

policeman

полицай

poli`tza

preacher

проповедник

propo`vedni

president

президент

prezi`den

representative

представител

pred`stavite

scientist

учен

`uche

secretary

секретарка

sekre`tark

singer

певец

pe`vet

soldier

войник

voy`ni

teacher

учител

u`chite

technician

техник

teh`ni

treasurer

касиер

kəsi`e

---

writer

писател

pi`sate

---

zoologist

зоолог

zoo`lo

Related Verbs

to deliver

доставям

dos`tavyə

---

to enjoy

наслаждавам се

nəsləzh`davəm s

---

to grow

раста

ras`t

---

to laugh

смея се

`smeya s

---

to love

обичам

o`bichə

to make

правя

`pravy

to manage

управлявам

uprəv`lyavə

to repair

поправям

pop`ravyə

to serve

служа

sluzh

to sing

пея

p`ey

to smile

усмихвам се

us`mihvəm s

to talk

говоря

go`vor

to think

мисля

`misly

---

to work

работя

rə`boty

---

to work at

работя в

rə`botya

---

to work for

работя за

rə`botya z

---

to work on

работя върху

rə`botya vər`h

---

to worship

боготворя

bogotvo`ry

---

to write

пиша

`pish

John is a successful **pilot** and **businessman**. This came as no surprise to any of his **family** and **friends**, but his start in life wasn't an easy one. When he was just a **baby**, John spent a lot of time seeing **doctors** for a rare condition he was born with. As an **infant**, he was very sick and required the care of a **nurse** all the time. While he was in the hospital, everyone came to visit him; **aunts**, **uncles**, **cousins**, and of course his **grandparents**. Finally, he got well and he was able to live a normal, healthy life. Because of all he had been through, his **parents** knew he would be a successful **man**. As a **toddler**, he and his **grandfather** loved to watch planes fly over his house. John's **grandfather** told his **grandson** that he could be anything he wanted when he grew up. He was such a curious **child**, but never lost his love of planes, he even dreamed of being an **astronaut**. As he grew older, he really excelled in math and science class, his **teachers** were amazed and his **mom** and **dad** were so proud of him. He was the top **student** in his class when he graduated high school. He was a **tall**, **handsome young man** with **black hair** and **blue eyes**. He was also very talented on the basketball court; his **coach** thought he was a fine **youth** as well. He was just a **teenager** when he finished college and became a **pilot**, finally getting to live his lifelong dream. One day there was an accident that forced John into the hospital for quite some time, there he met a young **woman** named Rachel, and she was a **nurse.** John quickly recovered under the care of his **girlfriend**, but he was never able to fly again. He did however become a flight school **instructor** where he was able to teach other people how to fly. It wasn't long that John and Rachel because **husband** and **wife.** They had two lovely **children**, one **boy** and one **girl.** Jill is quite the **singer**; everything is a microphone to this aspiring **rock star**. She is the cutest little **princess** you have ever seen! But Little Johnny Junior is following in his **father's** footsteps because he dreams of being a **pilot**, just like his **daddy. Father**, **son**, and **grandson** all love to spend quiet Sunday afternoons watching the planes go by. John knows that one day his **son** will be able to fly planes just like he did. While this thought scares him a little because of the accident, he is very proud of his **son** for his passion for flying. Maybe one day he will be a **student** in his **father's** flight school. In all of his successes, John's **family** is the achievement he is most proud of.

Джон е успешен **пилот** и **бизнесмен**. Това не беше изненада за никой от неговото **семейство** и **приятели**, но стартът му в живота не беше лесен. Когато беше още **бебе,** Джон прекарваше много време по **лекари** заради рядкото заболяване, с което беше роден. Като **бебе** той беше много болен и изискваше грижите на **медицинска сестра** през цялото време. Докато беше в болницата, всички идваха да го видят – **лели, чичовци, братовчеди** и разбира се, **баби и дядовци**. Накрая той се оправи и можеше да живее нормален, здравословен начин на живот. Заради всичко, през което е преминал, **родителите** му знаеха, че той ще бъде успешен **мъж**. Когато **прохождаше**, той и неговият **дядо** обичаха да гледат как самолетите летят над къщата му. **Дядото** на Джон каза на **внука** си, че може да стане какъвто си поиска, когато порасне. Той беше толкова любопитно **дете**, но никога не загуби любовта си към самолетите, дори мечтаеше да бъде **астронавт**. Когато порасна, той беше отличен **ученик** по математика и наука, **учителите** бяха изумени, а **майка** му и **баща** му бяха толкова горди с него. Той беше най-добрият **ученик** в класа си, когато завърши гимназия. Той беше **висок, красив млад мъж** с черна коса и **сини очи**. Той беше и много талантлив на баскетболното игрище; неговият **треньор** мислеше, че той е чудесен **младеж**. Беше **тийнейджър,** когато завърши колежа и стана **пилот**, най-накрая изживявайки мечтата на живота си. Един ден се случи инцидент, който принуди Джон да остане в болница доста време и там той срещна млада **жена** на име Рейчъл, която беше **медицинска сестра**. Джон бързо се възстанови под грижите на своята **приятелка**, но никога повече не можа да лети. Той обаче стана **инструктор** в училище за пилоти, където можеше да учи други хора как да летят. Не мина много време, преди Джон и Рейчъл да станат **съпруг** и **съпруга**. Те имаха две прекрасни **деца** – едно **момче** и едно **момиче**. Джил е голяма **певица**; всичко е микрофон за тази амбициозна **рок звезда**. Тя е най-сладката малка **принцеса**, която сте виждали! Но малкият Джони младши върви по стъпките на **баща** си, защото си мечтае да стане **пилот**, точно като своя **татко**. **Баща, син** и **дядо** обичат да прекарват тихи неделни следобеди, гледайки как самолетите отминават. Джон знае, че един ден неговият **син** ще може да управлява самолети точно като него. Макар че тази мисъл го плаши малко заради инцидента, той много се гордее със **сина** си заради страстта му по летенето. Може би един ден той ще бъде **ученик** в училището за пилоти на **баща** си. От целия си успех, Джон се гордее най-много със своето **семейството**.

4) Parts of the Body

ankle
глезен
`gleze

arm
ръка
rə`k

back
гръб
grʌ

beard
брада
brə`d

belly
корем
ko`re

blood
кръв
krʌ

body
тяло
`tyal

bone

кост

kos

brain

мозък

`mozə

breast

гърди

gər`d

buttocks

задник

`zadni

calf

прасец

prə`set

cheek

буза

`buz

chest

гръден кош

`grəden kos

chin

брадичка

brə`dichk

ear

ухо

u`h

elbow

лакът

`lakə

eye

око

o`k

eyebrow

вежда

`vezhd

eyelash

мигла

`migl

face

лице

li`ts

finger

пръст

prʌs

finger nail

нокът

`nokə

fist

юмрук

yum`ru

flesh

плът

plʌ

foot/feet

стъпало/стъпала

stə`palo/ stə`pal

forearm

ръка

rə`k

forehead

чело

che`l

hair

коса

ko`s

hand

ръка

rə`k

head

глава

glə`v

heart

сърце

sər`tz

heel

пета

pe`t

hip

бедро

bed`r

jaw

челюст

`chelyus

knee

коляно

ko`lyan

leg

крак

kra

lips

устни

`ustn

moustache

мустаци

mus`tatz

mouth

уста

us`t

---

muscle

мускул

`musku

---

nail

нокът

`nokə

---

neck

врат

vra

---

nose

нос

no

---

nostril

ноздра

`nozdr

---

palm

длан

dla

---

shin

пищял

pish`tya

---

shoulder

рамо

`ram

---

skin

кожа

`kozh

---

spine

гръбнак

grəb`na

---

stomach

стомах

sto`ma

---

teeth/tooth

зъб/зъби

zʌb/`zʌb

---

thigh

бедро

bed`r

---

throat

гърло

`gʌrl

---

thumb

палец

`palet

---

toe

пръст на крака

prʌst na krə`k

toenail

нокът на пръст на крака

`nokət na prʌst na krə`k

tongue

език

ezi

underarm

подмишница

pod`mishnitz

waist

кръст

krʌs

wrist

китка

`kitk

Related Verbs

to exercise

тренирам

tre`nirə

to feel

чувствам

`chuvstvə

---

to hear

чувам

`chuvə

---

to see

виждам

`vizhdə

---

to smell

помирисвам

pomi`risvə

---

to taste

вкусвам

`vkusvə

---

to touch

докосвам

do`kosvə

One day an alien crash landed on planet Earth. He was very confused and didn't know where he was. As he explored this undiscovered world, he happened along a little boy named David. David was eight years old and wasn't scared at all; after all, he knew there were aliens and he was happy to finally meet one. The alien had a large **head** and funny pointing **ears;** and he moved in a curious way with six **legs**! The alien was so confused when he saw the boy, so he asked David, "Why do you look so funny?" David laughed and told him all humans look like this. David has a good **heart** and wanted to make sure the alien was familiar with the people of Earth, so he told him all about how we use our body parts. "Let me tell you all about these funny parts", replied David. "On top of my body is my **head**; we have two **eyes** to see; two **ears** to hear; a **nose** to smell; and a **mouth** to talk and eat." The alien was surprised because he had all of these parts, but they looked much different. "Well then," said the alien, "what are those things you are standing on and why are there only two of them? David said, "These are **legs**, we just put one in front of the other and it makes us walk or run." The alien was amazed that the human could walk with only two **legs,** after all, he had six **legs** and he needed them all to get around! "What are those things that are dangling off your upper **legs**?" asked the alien. "Oh, these? They are called **fingers** and they are attached to my **hands** and **arms**. Look! Aren't they neat? I can wiggle them, tickle with them, I even use them to pick things up. They really come in handy for lots of different things." The alien really wanted a set of those fingers, and then to find out there are **toes** on the end of the **legs**... wow! He just had to have some! The alien wanted to know more, so he continued, "What is that stuff sticking up on the top of your **head**?" David replied, "That is called **hair.** It grows really fast, even after I cut it off, it just grows back out!! Adult humans have **hair** on other parts of their bodies; l**egs, arms, face,** even their **toes**!" "Why don't you have **hair** on those parts?" asked the alien. David told him that he would not grow **hair** on those parts until he grows up. The alien was satisfied with David's explanation of the human body parts and decided it was time to return home. David was sad to see him go, but so excited to tell his friends all about his encounter with such a curious alien.

Един ден катастрофирало извънземно се приземи на планетата Земя.То беше много объркано и не знаеше къде се намира. Докато изследваше този неоткрит свят, то се срещна с малко момче на име Дейвид. Дейвид беше на осем години и изобщо не се страхуваше. Той знаеше, че има извънземни и се радваше, че накрая срещна едно. Извънземното имаше голяма **глава** и смешни заострени **уши** и се движеше по любопитен начин с шест **крака!** Извънземното беше толкова объркано, когато видя момчето и попита Дейвид: „Защо изглеждаш толкова смешно?" Дейвид се засмя и му каза, че всички хора изглеждат така. Дейвид има добро **сърце** и искаше да се увери, че извънземното е запознато с хората на Земята, затова му каза как използваме частите на нашето тяло. „Нека ти разкажа всичко за тези смешни части", отговори Дейвид. „На върха на тялото ми е моята **глава;** ние имаме две **очи**, за да виждаме; две **уши**, за да чуваме; **нос,** за да помирисваме и **уста**, за да говорим и ядем." Извънземното беше изненадано, защото то имаше всичките тези части, но те изглеждаха много различно. „Е, каза извънземното, какви са тези неща, на които стоите и защо са само две?" Дейвид каза: „Това са **крака**, ние просто поставяме единия пред другия и така ходим или тичаме." Извънземното беше изумено, че хората могат да ходят само на два **крака**, а той имаше шест **крака** и всичките му трябваха, за да се разхожда! „Какви са тези неща, които висят от горните ви **крака?**" попита извънземното. „О, тези ли? Те се наричат **пръсти** и са закачени за моите **ръце.** Виж! Не са ли изящни? Мога да ги мърдам, гъделичкам, дори мога да ги използвам, за да вдигам неща. Те наистина са удобни за много различни неща." Извънземното много искаше комплект такива пръсти и тогава откри, че има **пръсти** в края на **краката**... еха! То искаше да има такива! Извънземното искаше да знае повече, затова продължи: „Какво е това нещо, което стърчи от **главата** ти?" Дейвид отговори: „Това се нарича **коса**. Тя расте много бързо и дори след като я срежа, тя пак пораства!! Възрастните хора имат **коса** и на други части от тялото си: **крака, ръце, лице** и дори **пръстите на краката!**" „Защо нямаш коса на тези части?" попита извънземното. Дейвид му каза, че няма да има **коса** на тези части докато не порасне. Извънземното беше доволно от обяснението на Дейвид за частите на човешкото тяло и реши, че е време да се върне вкъщи. На Дейвид му беше тъжно да го гледа как си отива, но беше толкова развълнуван да разкаже на приятелите си всичко за неговата среща с такова любопитно извънземно.

5) Animals

alligator

алигатор

əli`gato

anteater

мравояд

mrəvo`ya

antelope

антилопа

ənti`lop

ape

маймуна

may`mun

armadillo

броненосец

brone`noset

baboon

павиан

pəvi`a

bat

прилеп

`prile

bear

мечка

`mechk

---

beaver

бобър

`bobə

---

bison

бизон

bi`zo

---

bobcat

американски рис

əmeri`kanski ri

---

camel

камила

kə`mil

---

caribou

карибу

kəri`b

---

cat

котка

`kotk

---

chameleon

хамелеон

həmele`o

---

cheetah

гепард

ge`par

---

chipmunk

североамериканска катерица

severnoəmeri`kanskə `kateritz

---

cougar

пума

`pum

---

cow

крава

`krav

---

coyote

койот

ko`yo

---

crocodile

крокодил

kroko`di

---

deer

елен

el`e

---

dinosaur

динозавър

dinoza`və

---

dog

куче

`kuch

---

donkey

магаре

mə`gar

---

elephant

слон

slo

---

emu

ему

e`m

---

ferret

полуопитомен пор

po`lu`pitomen po

---

fox

лисица

li`sitz

---

frog

жаба

`zhab

---

gerbil

джербили

dzher`bil

---

giraffe

жираф

zhi`ra

---

goat

коза

ko`z

---

gorilla

горила

go`ril

---

groundhog

мармот

mər`mo

---

guinea pig

морско свинче

`morsko svin`ch

---

hamster

хамстер

`hamste

---

hedgehog

таралеж

tərə`lez

---

hippopotamus

хипопотам

hipopo`ta

---

horse

кон

ko

iguana

игуана

igu`an

kangaroo

кенгуру

`kengur

lemur

лемур

le`mu

leopard

леопард

leo`par

lion

лъв

lə

lizard

гущер

`gushte

llama

лама

`lam

meerkat
сурикат
suri`ka

mouse/mice
мишка/мишки
`mishkə/`mishk

mole
къртица
kər`titz

monkey
маймуна
məy`mun

moose
лос
lo

otter
видра
`vidr

panda
панда
`pand

panther
пантера
pən`ter

pig

прасе

prə`s

platypus

птицечовка

ptitze`chovk

polar bear

полярна мечка

po`lyarnə `mechkə

porcupine

бодливо прасе

bod`livo prə`s

rabbit

заек

`zae

raccoon

миеща мечка

`mieshtə `mechk

rat

плъх

plʌ

rhinoceros

носорог

noso`ro

sheep

овца

ov`tz

---

skunk

скункс

skunk

---

sloth

ленивец

le`nivet

---

snake

змия

zmi`y

---

squirrel

катерица

`kateritz

---

tiger

тигър

`tigə

---

toad

крастава жаба

`krastəvə `zhab

---

turtle

костенурка

koste`nurk

---

walrus

морж

morz

warthog

брадавичеста свиня

brə`davichestə svi`ny

weasel

невестулка

neves`tulk

wolf

вълк

vʌl

zebra

зебра

`zebr

Birds

canary

канарче

kə`narch

chicken

пиле

`pil

crow
гарван/врана
`garvən/`vran

dove
гълъб
`gʌlə

duck
патица
`patitz

eagle
орел
o`re

falcon
сокол
so`ko

flamingo
фламинго
flə`ming

goose
гъска
`gʌsk

hawk
ястреб
`yastre

hummingbird

колибри

ko`libr

---

ostrich

щраус

`shtrau

---

owl

бухал

`buhə

---

parrot

папагал

pəpə`ga

---

peacock

паун

`pau

---

pelican

пеликан

peli`ka

---

pheasant

фазан

fə`za

---

pigeon

гълъб

`gʌlə

---

robin
червеношийка
cherveno`shiyk

rooster
петел
pe`te

sparrow
врабче
vrəb`ch

swan
лебед
`lebe

turkey
пуйка
`puyk

Water/Ocean/Beach

бass
костур
kos`tu

catfish
сом
so

clam
мида
`mid

crab
рак
ra

goldfish
златна рибка
`zlatnə `ribk

jellyfish
медуза
me`duz

lobster
омар
o`ma

mussel
мида
`mid

oyster
стрида
`strid

salmon
сьомга
`syomg

shark
акула
ə`kul

trout
пъстърва
pəs`tʌrv

tuna
риба тон
`ribə to

whale
кит
ki

Insects

ant
мравка
`mravk

bee
пчела
pche`l

beetle
бръмбар
`brʌmbə

butterfly

пеперуда

pepe`rud

cockroach

хлебарка

hle`bark

dragonfly

водно конче

`vodno `konch

earthworm

дъждовен червей

dəzh`doven `cherve

flea

бълха

bəl`h

fly

муха

mu`h

gnat

комар

ko`ma

grasshopper

скакалец

skəkə`let

ladybug

калинка

kə`link

---

moth

молец

mo`let

---

mosquito

комар

ko`ma

---

spider

паяк

`paya

---

wasp

оса

o`s

Related Verbs

to eat

ям

ya

---

to bark

лая

`lay

---

to chase

преследвам

pres`ledvə

to feed

храня

`hrany

to hibernate

спя зимен сън

spya `zimen sʌ

to hunt

ловувам

lo`vuvə

to move

движа се

`dvizhə s

to perch

кацвам

`katzvə

to prey

плячкосвам

plyach`kosvə

to run

тичам

`tichə

to swim

плувам

`pluvə

---

to wag

въртя (опашка)

vər`tya (o`pashkə

---

to walk

вървя

vər`vy

Sarah is a seven year old girl who loves to visit the zoo. Her mom takes her to the local zoo at least once a week to see her favorite animals. This is an account of her usual visit to the zoo: When they arrive, they must pass by the **flamingos** and boy do they smell! They are pretty to look at, but don't get too close! Sarah insists that they visit her favorite animal first, the **elephants**. She loves how big, yet gentle they are. They spend time watching the **elephants** move about their habitat and one time, she even got to see an **elephant** paint! Next, they visit the Birds' Nest exhibit. They have many different species of **birds** on display, including **sparrows**, **robins**, **peacocks**, **canaries**, **hummingbirds**, they even have an **eagle**! The **eagle** is so majestic; it is Sarah's favorite **bird**. Sometimes the **eagle's** trainer will put on a show and Sarah just loves to see it spread its wings! After visiting the birds, Sarah likes to visit the mammal section of the zoo. They have **bears**, **tigers**, **lions**, **monkeys**, they even have **pandas**! One of the **pandas** had twin babies last year and Sarah has really enjoyed watching them grow up. After lunch, they visit the **reptile** house; there are lots of scaly looking animals there! The **alligators** are big and scary, but Sarah likes to watch from a distance. They also have **frogs** in lots of different colors; some are green, some are yellow and black, and some are blue! The best animals in the **reptile** house are the **snakes**. Some are stretched out long and some are coiled up taking a nap! They come in many different colors as well. Did you know that **snakes** eat **mice**? Sarah once got to see a **snake** eat its lunch, it was a little yucky to watch, but neat to see how a **snake** eats. After visiting the **reptiles**, Sarah and her mom go to see the **meerkats** and **warthogs**. They always make Sarah think of her favorite movie characters. The **meerkats** are silly little creatures and the **warthogs** just lay around in the mud all day! Sarah then goes to visit the tallest animal in the zoo, the **giraffe.** One day she even got to feed one! Its mouth is very weird to touch and it has a long tongue. One of the more popular sites at the zoo is the petting zoo. Sarah gets to brush the coat of **goats**, **sheep**, and even **pigs**! One last stop, to ride the train. While on the zoo train, Sarah gets to see lots of different animals, such as **kangaroos**, **ostriches**, **turtles**, and many more! Maybe one day, Sarah's mom can talk her into going to the aquarium instead of the zoo. Sarah would surely enjoy seeing **sharks**, **whales**, and **jellyfish**!

Сара е деветгодишно момиче, което обича да ходи в зоопарка. Майка ѝ я води в местния зоопарк поне веднъж седмично, за да види любимите си животни. Това е разказ за обикновеното ѝ посещение в зоопарка: Когато пристигнат, те трябва да минат покрай **фламингите,** а как миришат те! Те са красиви за гледане, но не се приближавайте прекалено много! Сара настоява първо да посетят любимото ѝ животно – **слоновете**. На нея ѝ харесва колко големи, но мили са те. Прекарват време да гледат как **слоновете** се движат в своя хабитат, а веднъж дори видя как един **слон** рисува! След това посещават изложбата Гнездото на птицата. Показани са много видове **птици,** включително **врабчета, червеношийки, канарчета, колибри** и дори има **орел**! **Орелът** е толкова величествен, той е любимата **птица** на Сара. Понякога дресьорът на **орела** изнася представление и Сара много обича да гледа как той си разперва крилата! След като посети птиците, Сара обича да посещава отдела с бозайници в зоопарка. Там има **мечки, тигри, лъвове, маймуни** и дори **панди**! Една от **пандите** имаше две бебета миналата година и Сара обичаше да ги гледа как растат. След обяда те посещават помещението с **влечуги,** там има много животни, покрити с люспи! **Алигаторите** са големи и страшни, но Сара обича да ги гледа от разстояние. Там има и **жаби** в много различни цветове – някои са зелени, други са жълти и черни, а някои са сини! Най-добрите животни в помещението с **влечуги** са **змиите**. Някои са дълги и разгънати, а други са навити и си подремват! Те също имат различни цветове. Знаехте ли, че **змиите** ядат **мишки**? Веднъж Сара видя как змиите обядват, беше малко гадно за гледане, но и хубаво да види как яде **змията**. След като посетят **влечугите**, Сара и майка ѝ отиват да видят **сурикатите** и **брадавичестите свине**. Те винаги карат Сара да си мисли за любимите ѝ герои от филми. **Сурикатите** са глупави малки същества, а **брадавичестите свине** просто се излежават в калта по цял ден! След това Сара отива да види най-високото животно в зоопарка – **жирафа**. Един ден тя дори нахрани един! Устата му е много странна за пипане и има дълъг език. Едно от най-популярните места в зоопарка е това, където е разрешено пипането на животните. Сара четка козината на **кози, овци** и дори **прасета**! Още една спирка - на влака. Докато се вози на влака в зоопарка, Сара вижда много различни животни, като **кенгура, щрауси, костенурки** и много други! Може би един ден майката на Сара ще я заведе в аквариума, вместо в зоопарка. На Сара със сигурност ще ѝ хареса да види **акули, китове** и **медузи!**

6) Plants and Trees

acacia
акация
ə`kaciy

acorn
жълъд
`zhələ

annual
едногодишно
ednogo`dishn

apple tree
ябълково дърво
`yabəlkovo dər`v

bamboo
бамбук
bəm`bu

bark
кора
ko`r

bean
боб
bo

berry

зрънце

`zrʌntz

birch

бреза

bre`z

blossom

цвят

tzvya

branch

клон

klo

brush

храсталак

hrəstə`la

bud

пъпка

`pʌpk

bulb

луковица

`lukovitz

bush

храст

hras

cabbage

зеле

`zel

cactus

кактус

`kaktu

carnation

карамфил

kərəm`fi

cedar

кедър

`kedə

cherry tree

черешово дърво

chere`shovo dər`v

chestnut

кестен

`keste

corn

царевица

`tzarevitz

cypress

кипарис

ki`pari

deciduous

широколистен

shiroko`liste

dogwood

кучешки дрян

`kucheshki drya

eucalyptus

евкалипт

evkə`lip

evergreen

вечнозелен

`vechno`zele

fern

папрат

`paprə

fertilizer

тор

to

fir

ела

e`l

flower

цвете

`tzvet

foliage
шума
`shum

---

forest
гора
go`r

---

fruit
плод
plo

---

garden
градина
gra`din

---

ginko
гинко
`gink

---

grain
зърно
`zərn

---

grass
трева
tre`v

---

hay
сено
se`n

---

herb
билка
`bilk

hickory
хикория
hi`koriy

ivy
бръшлян
brəsh`lya

juniper
хвойна
`hvoyn

kudzu
кудзу
`kudz

leaf/leaves
листо/листа
lis`to/lis`t

lettuce
маруля
mə`ruly

lily
лилия
`liliy

magnolia

магнолия

məg`noliy

---

maple tree

кленово дърво

`klenovo dər`v

---

moss

мъх

mʌ

---

nut

ядка

`yadk

---

oak

дъб

dʌ

---

palm tree

палма

`palm

---

pine cone

шишарка

shi`shark

---

pine tree

борче

`borch

---

plant

растение

rəs`teni

---

peach tree

праскова

`praskov

---

pear tree

круша

`krush

---

petal

венчелистче

`venchelistch

---

poison ivy

отровен бръшлян

ot`roven brəsh`lya

---

pollen

цветен прашец

`tzveten prə`shet

---

pumpkin

тиква

`tikv

---

root

корен

`kore

---

roses
рози
`roz`

sage
градински чай
grə`dinski cha

sap
мъзга
məz`g

seed
семе
`sem

shrub
храст
hras

squash
тиква
`tikv

soil
почва
`pochv

stem
стъбло
stəb`l

thorn

трън

trʌ

---

tree

дърво

dər`v

---

trunk

дънер

`dʌne

---

vegetable

зеленчук

zelen`chu

---

vine

лоза

lo`z

---

weed

плевел

`pleve

Related Verbs

to fertilize

торя

to`ry

---

to gather

събирам

sə`birə

---

to grow

отглеждам

ot`glezhdə

---

to harvest

жъна

`zhʌn

---

to pick

бера

be`r

---

to plant

садя

sə`dy

---

to plow

ора

o`r

---

to rake

греба

gre`b

---

to sow

сея

`sey

to spray

пръскам

`prʌskə

---

to water

поливам

po`livə

---

to weed

плевя

ple`vy

Farmer Smith was a kind old man. He ran the local farm and orchard. One day, while out harvesting **corn**, a bird hobbled over and sat down beside him. Farmer Smith noticed the poor little bird had a broken wing, so he gathered up his supplies and cradled the bird in one of his baskets. The bird could not fly and was helpless, so Farmer Smith decided to nurse the bird back to good health. He used a small piece of **bark** to bandage the broken wing. Every day Farmer Smith would take the bird for a walk and they would rest against the **trunk** of an old **oak tree** at the edge of the property. The farmer loved to tell the bird all about the different **plants** on his farm. He told of the **pine trees** that lined his property. These **trees** were perfect Christmas **trees**. He told of the **flowers** that grew wild near the lake, he explained how they started as a seed, and then grew into a bulb, then eventually into a beautiful **flower**. They were so colorful and vibrant; they remind the farmer of his wife. He would bring her **roses** every day for her to use on the dinner table. His wife was a wonderful cook, she could cook anything that the farmer grew; **squash, pumpkin, pears, apples, cabbage,** and many more. The way she used the **herbs** was like magic! The little bird loved to hear the stories about the farmer's wife, just hearing about her brought the bird comfort. One day, while the farmer was out **tilling** the **soil,** he heard a small sound approaching him; he turned around to see it was the little bird he had been caring for. She had learned to fly again! The farmer decided it was time for the bird to go live in the **forest** again. She was strong enough and prepared to survive on her own. It was a sad day, but the farmer took the bird into the **deciduous forest** and released her. One day, in early spring the farmer noticed a bird on his window sill. He couldn't believe his eyes, it was the same bird. He was so pleased to see the bird again, for it reminded him of his wife. Now, every spring, the bird comes to visit the farmer. He and the bird go to that old **oak tree** and Farmer Smith tells a new story about his wife. I don't know whatever happened to that bird, but it visited the farmer every year until the farmer passed away. It even visited his window sill at the hospital the year before he died. No one has ever seen it happen, but I know that the bird brings a single **rose** to Farmer Brown's resting site. Some may see the bird as a small, helpless creature, but for Farmer Smith, the bird helped to fill a void for his remaining years.

Фермерът Смит беше добър старец. Той управляваше местна ферма и овощна градина. Един ден, докато прибираше **царевица**, една птица докоцука и седна до него. Фермерът Смит забеляза, че крилото на бедната птица е счупено, затова той събра своите припаси и сложи птицата в една от своите кошници. Птицата не можеше да лети и беше безпомощна, затова фермерът Смит реши да се грижи за нея, докато оздравее. Той използва малко парче **кора**, за да превърже счупеното ѝ крило. Всеки ден фермерът Смит водеше птицата на разходка и те си почиваха на **дънера** на един **дъб** в края на имота. Фермерът обичаше да разказва на птицата за различните **растения** във фермата му. Той разказа за **борчетата**, които ограждаха неговия имот. Тези **дървета** бяха идеални коледни **дървета**. Той разказа за дивите **цветя**, които растяха край езерото, обясни как те започнаха като семена, превърнаха се в луковици, а накрая и в красиви **цветя**. Те бяха толкова цветни и изпълнени с живот; напомняха на фермера за жена му. Той ѝ носеше **рози** всеки ден, за да ги слага на масата за вечеря. Съпругата му беше отлична готвачка – тя можеше да сготви всичко, което фермерът отглеждаше: **тикви, круши, ябълки, зеле** и много други. Начинът, по който използваше **билките**, беше магически! Малката птица обичаше да слуша историите за съпругата на фермера, самото слушане я утешаваше. Един ден, докато фермерът беше навън да **обработва почвата**, той чу приближаващ се звук. Той се обърна и видя, че това е малката птичка, за която се грижеше. Тя се беше научила да лети отново! Фермерът реши, че беше време птицата да отлети отново в **гората**. Тя беше достатъчно силна и готова да оцелее сама. Беше тъжен ден, но фермерът заведе птицата в **широколистната гора** и я освободи. Един ден в ранната пролет фермерът забеляза птица на перваза на прозореца си. Той не можеше да повярва на очите си – това беше същата птица. Той беше толкова щастлив да види птицата отново, тъй като тя му напомняше за съпругата му. Сега всяка пролет птицата идваше да посети фермера. Тя и фермерът отиваха при стария **дъб** и фермерът Смит разказваше нова история за жена си. Не знам какво стана с тази птица, но тя посещаваше фермера всяка година до смъртта му. Тя дойде и на перваза на прозореца в болницата в годината, преди той да почине. Никой не го е видял, но аз знам, че птицата носи по една **роза** на гроба на фермера Смит. За някои птицата може да е малко, беззащитно създание, но тя помогна на фермера Смит да запълни една празнота в последните си години.

7) Meeting Each Other

Greetings/Introductions:

Good morning
Добро утро
`dobro `utr

Good afternoon
Добър ден
`dobər de

Good evening
Добър вечер
`dobər `veche

Good night
Лека нощ
`lekə nosh

Hi
Здрасти
`zdrast

Hello
Здравей
zdrə`ve

Have you met (name)?
Познаваш ли (име)?
poz`navəsh li m

Haven't we met?

Не сме ли се срещали?

ne sme li se `shreshtəl

How are you?

Как си?

kak s

How are you today?

Как си днес?

kak si dne

How do you do?

Как си? / Приятно ми е

pri`yatno mi

How's it going?

Как върви?

kak vər`v

I am (name)

Казвам се (име)

`kazvam se (`ime

I don't think we've met.

Не мисля, че сме се срещали.

ne `misya che sme se `sreshtəl

It's nice to meet you.

Радвам се да се запознаем.

`radvəm se da se zəpoz`nae

Meet (name)

Запознай се с (име)

zəpoz`nay se s (`ime

My friends call me (nickname)

Приятелите ми викат (прякор)

pri`yatelite mi `vikət (`pryakor

My name is (name)

Името ми е (име)

`imeto mi

Nice to meet you

Радвам се да се запознаем

`radvəm se da se zəpoz`nae

Nice to see you again.

Радвам се да те видя отново.

`radvəm se da te `vidya ot`nov

Pleased to meet you.

Приятно ми е да се запознаем.

pri`yatno mi e da se zəpoz`nae

This is (name)

Това е (име)

to`va e (`ime

What's your name?

Как се казваш?

kak se `kazvəs

Who are you?

Кой си ти?

`koy si t

Greeting Answers

Fine, thanks

Добре, благодаря

`dobre bləgodə`ry

I'm exhausted

Изтощен съм

iztosh`ten sə

I'm okay

Добре съм

`dobre sə

I'm sick

Болен съм

`bolen sə

I'm tired

Уморен съм

umo`ren sə

Not too bad

Не е зле

ne e zl

Not too well, actually

Всъщност не толкова добре

`vsʌshtnost ne `tolkovə dob`r

Very well

Много добре

`mnogo dob`r

Saying Goodbye

Bye

Чао

`cha

Good bye

Довиждане

do`vizhdən

Good night

Лека нощ

`lekə nosh

See you

До скоро

do `skor

See you later

Ще се видим по-късно

shte se `vidim po-`kʌsn

See you next week

До другата седмица

do `drugətə `sedmitz

See you soon

До скоро виждане

do `skoro `vizhdən

See you tomorrow

До утре

do `utr

Courtesy

Excuse me

Извинете

izvi`net

Pardon me

Извинете

izvi`net

I'm sorry

Съжалявам

səzhə`lyavə

Thanks

Благодаря

bləgodər`y

Thank you
Благодаря ви
bləgodər`ya v

You're welcome
Моля / Няма защо
`molya/`nyamə zə`sht

Special Greetings

Congratulations
Поздравления
pozdrəv`leniy

Get well soon
Оправяй се по-бързо
op`ravyay se po-`bʌzr

Good luck
Успех
us`pe

Happy New Year
Честита нова година
ches`titə `novə go`din

Happy Easter
Честито Възкресение
ches`tito vəzkre`seni

Merry Christmas

Весела Коледа

`veselə `koled

Well done

Браво

`brav

Related Verbs

to greet

поздравявам

pozdrə`vyavə

---

to meet

запознавам се с

zəpoz`navəm s

---

to say

казвам

`kazvə

---

to shake hands

ръкувам се

rə`kuvəm s

---

to talk

говоря

go`vory

---

to thank

благодаря

blagodar`y

This is the story of a man named Pop. He just started a new job as a greeter at the local discount store. His son was so proud, he gave him a card that said, "**Congratulations**". He is a little nervous because he has never been a store greeter before. Throughout the day, there are so many customers going in and out of the store, sometimes Pop forgets what he should say. "**Pleased to meet you**" or "**Can I help you out?**" are good options for being polite. His manager assured him, saying, "You will be just fine, so don't worry." He begins the work day with a smile on his face, but by the end of the day, his smile is erased. "**Good morning,**" he says with a smile to the nice lady walking down the produce aisle. "**How are you doing?**" asked Pop, but she must not have heard him, because she didn't stop to say **hello**. "Hmm", said Pop, I guess she didn't hear me because a polite person would have said something like, '**Fine, how are you?**' or '**I'm fine, thank you.**' Next there was man with a bushy white beard, he looked very friendly and kind. Pop greeted him politely and said, "**Happy New Year!**" The man just grunted and went on his way, I guess he wasn't friendly after all. Pop replied, "**Have a good day!**" The next several customers were polite and spoke to him. Some of the customers said, "**How do you do?**" and one said, "**My name is Jim. What is your name?**" As the day went on, Pop got really tired and his **greetings** were losing not seeming as effective as earlier in the day. His manager was upset, but gave him another chance. He warned Pop that just saying "**Hi**" or "**Hello**" wasn't enough for the friendly environment our customers are used to. "If you want to make a good impression, you have to be polite. You can say something like, '**Merry Christmas**' or '**Good day to you, sir**', but please be nice to everyone you meet. Finally, as the end of the day was nearing, Pop was very happy to finally be able to say, "**Good night**." He went home without his smile, but said tomorrow is a new day and I will make sure to smile for everyone.

Това е историята на мъж на име Поп. Той току-що започна нова работа като човек, който посреща гостите в местния дисконтен магазин. Синът му беше толкова горд – той му даде карта с надпис „**Поздравления**". Той е малко напрегнат, защото досега никога не е работил такова нещо. През деня има толкова много клиенти, които влизат и излизат от магазина, че понякога Поп забравя какво трябва да каже. „**Приятно ми е да се запознаем**" или „**Мога ли да ви помогна?**" са добри варианти да бъдете учтиви. Неговият мениджър го успокои, казвайки: „Ще се справиш, така че не се тревожи". Той започва работния ден с усмивка на лице, но до края на деня усмивката му изчезва. „**Добро утро**" каза той с усмивка на приятна дама, която върви между щандовете с плодове и зеленчуци. „**Как сте?**", попита Поп, но тя може би не го чу, защото не спря да го **поздрави**. „Хм", каза Поп, предполагам, че не ме чула, защото учтивият човек би казал нещо като „**Добре, а вие как сте?**" или „**Добре съм, благодаря**". После имаше един мъж с гъста бяла брада, който изглеждаше много любезен и вежлив. Поп го поздрави любезно и каза „**Честита нова година!**" Мъжът просто изсумтя и продължи по пътя си, предполагам, че все пак не беше любезен. Поп отвърна: „**Приятен ден!**" Следващите няколко клиенти бяха любезни и говориха с него. Някои от клиентите казаха: „**Как сте?**", а един каза: „**Казвам се Джим. А вие как се казвате?**" С напредването на деня Поп наистина се измори и неговите **поздрави** изглежда не бяха толкова ефективни, колкото в началото на деня. Мениджърът му беше разстроен, но му даде още един шанс. Той предупреди Поп, че казването просто на „**Здрасти**" или „**Здравейте**" не е достатъчно за приятелската атмосфера, с която са свикнали клиентите. „Ако искаш да направиш добро впечатление, трябва да бъдеш учтив. Може да кажеш нещо като „**Весела Коледа**" или „**Добър ден, господине**", но моля те бъди любезен с всеки, когото срещнеш. Накрая, когато краят на деня наближаваше, Поп беше много щастлив, че може да каже „**Лека нощ**". Той се прибра вкъщи без своята усмивка, но каза, че утре е нов ден и ще се постарае да се усмихва на всички.

8) House

air conditioner

климатик

klimə`ti

appliances

уреди

`ured

attic

таван

tə`va

awning

тента

`tent

backyard

заден двор

`zaden dvo

balcony

балкон

bəl`ko

basement

мазе

mə`z

bathroom

баня

`bany

---

bath tub

вана

`van

---

bed

легло

leg`l

---

bedroom

спалня

`spalny

---

blanket

одеяло

ode`yal

---

blender

блендер

`blende

---

blinds

щори

`shtor

---

bookshelf/bookcase

етажерка

etə`zherk

---

bowl

купа

`kup

---

cabinet

шкаф

shka

---

carpet

килим

ki`li

---

carport

навес

`nave

---

ceiling

таван

tə`va

---

cellar

изба

`izb

---

chair

стол

sto

---

chimney

комин

ko`mi

---

clock

часовник

chə`sovni

---

closet

килер

ki`le

---

computer

компютър

kom`pyutə

---

couch

канапе

kənə`p

---

counter

бар

ba

---

crib

детско креватче

`detsko kre`vatch

---

cupboard

бюфет

byu`fe

---

cup

чаша

cha`sh

---

curtain

завеса

zə`ves

---

desk

бюро

byu`r

---

dining room

столова

stolo`v

---

dishes

чинии

chi`ni

---

dishwasher

съдомиялна

sədomi`yaln

---

door

врата

vrə`t

---

doorbell

звънец

zvə`net

---

doorknob

дръжка на врата

`drəzhkə nə vrə`t

---

doorway

вход

vho

drapes

завеси

zə`ves

drawer

чекмедже

chekme`dzh

driveway

алея за коли към къща

ə`leya zə koli kəm `kʌsht

dryer

сушилня

su`shilny

duct

канал

kə`na

exterior

екстериор

eksteri`o

family room

всекидневна

vseki`dnevn

fan

вентилатор

venti`lato

---

faucet

кранче

`kranch

---

fence

ограда

og`rad

---

fireplace

камина

kə`min

---

floor

под

po

---

foundation

основа

os`nov

---

frame

рамка

`ramk

---

freezer

фризер

`frize

---

furnace

пещ

pesh

furniture

мебели

`mebel

garage

гараж

gə`raz

garden

градина

grə`din

grill

грил

gri

gutters

олуци

o`lutz

hall/hallway

коридор

kori`do

hamper

кош за пране

kosh zə prə`n

heater

печка

`pechk

---

insulation

изолация

izo`laciy

---

jacuzzi tub

джакузи

dzhə`kuz

---

key

ключ

klyuc

---

kitchen

кухня

`kuhny

---

ladder

стълба

`stəlb

---

lamp

лампа

`lamp

---

landing

стълбищна площадка

`stʌlbishtnə plo`shtadk

---

laundry

пране

prə`n

lawn

ливада

li`vad

lawnmower

косачка

ko`sachk

library

библиотека

biblio`tek

light

осветление

osvet`leni

linen closet

гардероб за бельо

gərde`rob zə be`ly

living room

хол

ho

lock

катинар

kəti`na

loft
таван
tə`va

mailbox
пощенска кутия
`poshtenskə ku`tiy

mantle
рамка на камина
`ramkə nə kə`min

master bedroom
основна спалня
os`novnə `spalny

microwave
микровълнова
mikro`vʌlnov

mirror
огледало
ogle`dal

neighborhood
квартал
kvər`ta

nightstand
нощно шкафче
`noshtno `shkafch

office
офис
ofi

oven
фурна
`furn

painting
картина
kər`tin

paneling
ламперия
ləm`periy

pantry
килерче за провизии
ki`lerche za pro`vizi

patio
вътрешен двор
`vʌtreshen dvo

picnic table
маса за пикник
`masə za `pikni

picture
картина
kər`tink

picture frame
рамка за картина
`ramkə zə kər`tin

---

pillow
възглавница
vəz`glavnitz

---

plates
чинии
chi`ni

---

plumbing
водопровод
vodopro`vo

---

pool
басейн
bə`sey

---

porch
веранда
ve`rand

---

queen bed
легло персон и половина
leg`lo per`son i polo`vin

---

quilt
юрган
yur`ga

railing

парапет

pərə`pe

---

range

готварска печка

got`varskə `pechk

---

refrigerator

хладилник

hlə`dilni

---

remote control

дистанционно

distəntzi`onn

---

roof

покрив

`pokri

---

room

стая

`stay

---

rug

килим

ki`li

---

screen door

врата с мрежа

vrə`ta s `mrezh

---

shed

барака

bə`rak

---

shelf/shelves

рафт/рафтове

raft/`raftov

---

shingle

битумна керемида

`bitumna kere`mid

---

shower

душ

dus

---

shutters

щори

`shtor

---

siding

облицовка

obli`tzovk

---

sink

мивка

`mivk

---

sofa

диван

di`va

---

stairs/staircase

стълби/стълбище

`stʌlbi/`stʌlbisht

step

стъпало

stə`pal

stoop

покрито преддверие

pok`rito pred`dveri

stove

печка

`pechk

study

кабинет

kəbi`ne

table

маса

`mas

telephone

телефон

tele`fo

television

телевизия

tele`viziy

toaster

тостер

`toste

---

toilet

тоалетна

toə`letn

---

towel

кърпа

`kʌrp

---

trash can

кош за боклук

kosh zə bok`lu

---

trim

перваз

per`va

---

upstairs

на горния етаж

nə `gorniya e`taz

---

utility room

мокро помещение

`mokro pomesh`teni

---

vacuum

прахосмукачка

prəhosmu`kachk

---

vanity

тоалетка

toə`letk

---

vase

ваза

`vaz

---

vent

отдушник

ot`dushni

---

wall

стена

ste`n

---

wardrobe

гардероб

gərde`ro

---

washer/washing machine

пералня

pe`ralny

---

waste basket

кошче за боклук

`koshche za bok`lu

---

water heater

бойлер

`boile

---

welcome mat

изтривалка

iztri`valk

---

window

прозорец

pro`zoret

---

window pane

стъкло на прозорец

stə`klo na pro`zoret

---

window sill

перваз на прозорец

per`vaz na pro`zoret

---

yard

двор

dvo

Related Verbs

to build

строя

stro`y

---

to buy

купувам

kupu`va

---

to clean

чистя

`chisty

---

to decorate

украсявам

ukrə`syavə

---

to leave

напускам

na`puskə

---

to move in

нанасям се

na`nasyəm s

---

to move out

изнасям се

iz`nasyəm s

---

to renovate

ремонтирам

remon`tirə

---

to repair

поправям

pop`ravya

---

to sell

продавам

pro`davə

---

to show

показвам

po`kazvə

---

to view

гледам

`gledə

---

to visit

посещавам

pose`shtavə

---

to work

работя

rə`boty

Mike and Linda just bought their first **house**. It is a not a large house, but it is very cozy. It is in a very nice **neighborhood** and has a cute, well-manicured **lawn**. It has a small front **porch**, which will be nice to relax on in the evenings after work. The **exterior** is light blue with a dark blue **door** and **shutters**. It has a nice size **garage** that is big enough for both of their cars and a small **shed** out back for their lawnmower. The **backyard** is small, but has a cute little swing set. One day, maybe they will have kids to enjoy it. The **living room** is very spacious and is beautifully decorated in greens and blues. The **walls** are painted light blue and the **curtains** are patterned green and blue. The **couch** and **chair** are very comfortable and roomy enough for the few guests they may have on occasion. Mike is very excited about the new **television** they had installed on the **wall** above the **fireplace**. The **kitchen** is small, yet functional. It has a **refrigerator**, a

dishwasher, an **oven**, and a built-in **microwave.** There is not much storage, so Linda will have to be very organized. The **walls** are painted yellow and it has a nice floral border. Linda did not pick it out, but it suits her taste well. The **house** has three **bedrooms**, which gives their family room to grow. The **master bedroom** is big enough to fit their **queen bed**, two **nightstands**, and a **dresser**. Linda has already picked out **curtains** to match the bedding. The **walls** are painted beige, but Linda thinks she can brighten the **room** with other decor. Linda's favorite part of the house is the master **bathroom**; it has a jacuzzi **tub** and she can't wait to try it out. It also has a separate **shower** and a double **vanity**. Mike works from home, so he plans to use one of the other, even smaller **bedrooms** as a home **office**. There is not a lot of space, but enough for his **desk**, **computer**, and a **bookshelf**. The back **porch** is nice and has a charcoal **grill** and a **picnic table.** Mike loves to cook on the **grill**, so it will be put to good use. They will need to get a **washing machine** and **dryer** for the **laundry room,** it is small, but it has a **sink**, which is very helpful when washing clothes. Overall, Mike and Linda picked out an excellent first home. It fits their budget, as well as their taste perfectly!

Майк и Линда тъкмо си купиха първата си **къща**. Тя не е голяма, но е много уютна. Тя е в много хубав **квартал** и има сладка, добре поддържана **ливада**. Има малка предна **веранда**, която е подходяща за почивка вечер след работа. **Екстериорът** е светлосин с тъмносини **врата** и **щори**. Тя има **гараж** с добър размер, който е достатъчно голям и за двете им коли и малка барака отзад за тяхната **косачка. Задният двор** е малък, но има сладки малки люлки. Един ден може би те ще имат деца, които да им се наслаждават. **Холът** е много просторен и е красиво боядисан в зелено и синьо. **Стените** са боядисани в светлосиньо, а **завесите** са със сини и зелени шарки. **Канапето** и **столовете** са много удобни и достатъчно широки за гостите, които може да имат по някакъв повод. Майк е много развълнуван за новия **телевизор**, който инсталираха на **стената** над **камината**. **Кухнята** е малка, но функционална. Тя има **хладилник, съдомиялна, фурна** и вградена **микровълнова**. Няма много място за съхранение, така че Линда трябва да е много организирана. **Стените** са боядисани в жълто и имат красива флорална ивица. Линда не я е избрала, но тя отговаря на вкуса ѝ. **Къщата** има три **спални**, което дава възможност на семейството им да расте. **Основната спалня** е достатъчно голяма, за да побере тяхното **легло персон и половина**, две **нощни шкафчета** и **скрин**. Линда вече е избрала **завеси**, които да отиват на завивките. **Стените** са боядисани в бежово, но Линда смята, че може да освежи **стаята** с друг цвят. Любимата част от къщата на Линда е основната **баня**; тя има **джакузи** и Линда няма търпение да го пробва. Тя има и отделен **душ** и двойна **тоалетка**. Майк работи от вкъщи, затова планува да използва една от другите по-малки **спални** за домашен **офис**. Няма много пространство, но е достатъчно за неговото **бюро, компютър** и **етажерка**. Задната **веранда** е хубава, има **грил** на въглища и **маса за пикник**. Майк много обича да готви на **грила**, така че той ще се използва много. Те ще трябва да си купят **пералня** и **сушилня** за **пералното помещение**, то е малко, но има **мивка**, което е много полезно за пране на дрехите. Като цяло, Майк и Линда избраха отличен първи дом. Той идеално отговаря на техния бюджет, както и на вкуса им!

9) Arts & Entertainment

3-D
3-D
tri d

---

action movie
екшън
`ekshə

---

actor/actress
актьор/актриса
ək`tyor/ək`tris

---

album
албум
əl`bu

---

alternative
алтернатива
əlternə`tiv

---

amphitheater
амфитеатър
`amfite`atə

---

animation
анимация
əni`maciy

---

artist
художник
hu`dozhni

audience
публика
`publik

ballerina
балерина
bəle`rin

ballet
балет
bə`le

band
група
`grup

blues
блус
blu

caption
надпис
`nadpi

carnival
карнавал
kərnə`va

cast
актьорски състав
әk`tyorski sәs`ta

choreographer
хореограф
horeo`gra

cinema
кино
`kin

classic
класика
`klasik

comedy
комедия
ko`mediy

commercial
реклама
rek`lam

composer
композитор
kompo`zito

concert
концерт
kon`tzer

conductor

диригент

diri`gen

---

contemporary

съвременен

səv`remene

---

country

държава

dər`zhav

---

credits

кредити

`kredit

Dancer

танцьор

tan`tzyor

---

director

режисьор

rezhi`syo

---

documentary

документален филм

dokumen`talen fi

---

drama

драма

`dram

---

drummer
барабанист
bərəbə`nis

duet
дует
du`e

episode
епизод
epi`zo

event
събитие
sə`biti

exhibit
експонат
ekspo`na

exhibition
изложба
iz`lozhb

fair
панаир
pənə`i

fantasy
фантастика
fən`tastik

feature/feature film
игрален филм
ig`ralen fil

film
филм
fil

flick
филм
fil

folk
народен
nə`rode

gallery
галерия
gə`leriy

genre
жанр
zhan

gig
ангажимент (на музикант и пр.)
əngəzhi`men

group
група
`grup

guitar

китара

ki`tar

---

guitarist

китарист

kitə`ris

---

hip-hop

хип-хоп

`hip - `ho

---

horror

ужаси

`uzhəs

---

inspirational

вдъхновяващ

vdəhno`vyavəsh

---

jingle

лесно запомняща се мелодия

`lesno zə`pomnyəshtə se me`lodiy

---

legend

легенда

le`gend

---

lyrics

текст на песен

teskt na `pese

---

magician

магьосник

mə`gyosni

microphone

микрофон

mikro`fo

motion picture

филм

fil

movie director

филмов режисьор

`filmov rezhi`syo

movie script

сценарий на филм

stze`nariy na fil

museum

музей

mu`ze

music

музика

`muzik

musical

мюзикъл

`myuzikə

musician

музикант

muzi`kan

mystery

мистерия

mis`teriy

new age

нова епоха

`novə e`poh

opera

опера

`oper

opera house

опера

`oper

orchestra

оркестър

or`kestə

painter

художник

hu`dozhni

painting

картина

kər`tin

parade

парад

pə`ra

performance

представление

predstə`vleni

pianist

пианист

piə`nis

picture

картина

kər`tin

play

пиеса

pi`es

playwright

драматург

drəmə`tur

pop

поп

po

popcorn

пуканки

`pukənk

producer

продуцент

produ`tzen

---

rap

рап

rap

---

reggae

реге

`reg

---

repertoire

репертоар

reperto`a

---

rock

рок

ro

---

role

роля

`roly

---

romance

романс

ro`man

---

scene

сцена

`stzen

---

science fiction

научна фантастика

nə`uchna fən`tastik

---

sculptor

скулптор

`skulpto

---

shot

кадър

`kadə

---

show

шоу

`sho

---

show business

шоу бизнес

`shou `bizne

---

silent film

ням филм

nyam fil

---

singer

певец

pe`vet

---

sitcom

ситком

`sitko

soloist

солист

so`lis

---

song

песен

`pese

---

songwriter

автор на песни

`avtor nə `pesn

---

stadium

стадион

stədi`o

---

stage

сцена

`stzen

---

stand-up comedy

стендъп комедия

`stendəp ko`mediy

---

television

телевизия

tele`viziy

TV show

ТВ шоу

`tivi `sho

---

theater
театър
te`atə

---

understudy
дубльор
dub`lyo

---

vocalist
вокал
vo`ka

---

violinist
цигулар
tzigu`la

Related Verbs

to act
играя
ig`ray

---

to applaud
аплодирам
əplo`dirə

---

to conduct
дирижирам
diri`zhirə

---

to dance
танцувам
tən`tzuvə

---

to direct
режисирам
rezhisi`rə

---

to draw
привличам
pri`vlichəm

---

to entertain
забавлявам
zəbəv`lyavə

---

to exhibit
излагам
iz`lagə

---

to host
домакин съм
domə`kim sə

---

to paint
рисувам
ri`suvə

---

to perform
изпълнявам
izpəl`nyavə

---

to play

играя

ig`ray

---

to sculpt

извайвам

iz`vayvə

---

to show

показвам

po`kazvə

---

to sing

пея

p`ey

---

to star

играя главна роля

ig`raya `glavnə `roly

---

to watch

гледам

`gledə

Mark Jones is a **legend** in **show business**. His career has been nothing less than amazing. He is an award-winning **actor, director**, and **producer** of **film** and **television**. Jones was born in West Central, California. His mother was a teacher and his father was a police officer. He came from humble beginnings and built his career from the bottom up. As a boy, he loved to be the center of attention; he either had a **microphone** in his hand or a **guitar** over his shoulder. He was a very talented **musician** and it seemed he was headed on a path towards becoming a **singer**. He is a talented **songwriter** as well. Few people know that he released his first and only **album** when he was just 16 years old. It was a **pop album**, but It didn't have much success. That didn't stop him from finding his purpose. He also tried **stand-up comedy**. He always drew large crowds, but he knew that wasn't what he was called to do. When he was in his early twenties, he decided to try out for the local community **musical**. He was amazing in his **role** and that is when he made the decision to try acting and he has never looked back! His acting career took off fast. He got his start on a **sitcom** called *Best Friends*. That show was very popular and aired for eight full seasons. It was the beginning of Jones' long and successful and career. He went on to star in several **feature films,** such as *The Dollar*, *Money Maze*, and *Backyard Boys*, just to name a few. There were a few flops in his career, but that didn't stop him. He has starred in many different **genres** of films; proving his versatility as an **actor**. He has played in **dramas, comedies**, and **documentaries**. He has also won multiple major awards for his acting. As time went on, he decided to try **directing films**. He was amazing as a **director** and won awards for his work with **feature films**, such as *The Child* and *End of All*. But that wasn't enough for Mark; he became a **producer** and to no surprise, was very successful. His **films** have been wildly successful and it makes everyone wonder where he will go next. It is safe to call Mark Jones a mega-**star**. He has not only been successful in every **entertainment** venture he has attempted, he has also been successful with his family. He has been married to his wife for twenty-five years, which is a rarity in show business.

Марк Джоунс е **легенда** в **шоу бизнеса**. Неговата кариера е чисто и просто невероятна. Той е награждаван **актьор, режисьор** и **продуцент** на филми и в телевизията. Джоунс е роден в Уест Сентръл, Калифорния. Майка му е учителка, а баща му – полицай. Той е от скромен произход и изгражда кариерата си от дъното. Като момче той обича да бъде център на вниманието; той е или с **микрофон** в ръка или с **китара** през рамо. Той е много талантлив **музикант** и изглежда е вървял към това да стане **певец**. Той е и талантлив **автор на песни**. Малко хора знаят, че той пуска първия си **албум**, когато е на 16 години. Това е **поп албум,** но не е много успешен. Това не го спира да открие целта си. Той е опитвал и **стендъп комедия**. Винаги е привличал големи тълпи, но е знаел, че не за това е призван. В началото на двайсетте си години решава да опита в местен **мюзикъл**. Невероятен е в своята **роля** и това решава да играе, като никога не поглежда назад! Кариерата му на актьор потръгва бързо. Той започва в **ситком**, наречен *Best Friends*. Това шоу е много популярно и се излъчва в цели осем сезона. Това е началото на дългата и успешна кариера на Джоунс. Той участва в няколко **играли филма**, като *The Dollar, Money Maze, Backyard Boys* и други. Има и няколко провала в неговата кариера, но това не го спира. Той участва в главната роля в много различни **жанрове** филми, което доказва неговата многостранност като **актьор**. Той играе в **драми, комедии** и **документални филми**. Печелил е и множество големи награди за играта си. С течение на времето той решава да опита да **режисира филми**. Невероятен е като **режисьор** и печели награди за своята работа с **играли филми**, като *The Child* и *End of All*. Но това не е достатъчно за Марк – той става **продуцент** и е много успешен, което не е изненадващо. Неговите **филми** са невероятно успешни и всички се чудят какво ще направи след това. Можем да наречем Марк Джоунс мега **звезда**. Той е успешен не само във всяко свое начинание в областта на **забавлението**, но и в своето семейство. Той е женен за съпругата си от двайсет и пет години, което е рядкост в шоу бизнеса.

10) Games and Sports

ace
ас
a

amateur
аматьор
amǝ`tyo

archery
стрелба с лък
strel`ba s lǝ

arena
арена
ǝ`ren

arrow
стрела
stre`l

athlete
атлет
ǝt`le

badminton
бадминтон
`badminto

ball

топка

`topk

---

base

база

`baz

---

baseball

бейзбол

`beyzbo

---

basket

кош

kos

---

basketball

баскетбол

`basketbo

---

bat

бухалка

bu`halk

---

bicycle

колело

kole`l

---

billiards

билярд

bi`lyar

---

bow

лък

lʌ

---

bowling

боулинг

`boulin

---

boxing

бокс

bok

---

captain

капитан

kəpi`ta

---

champion

шампион

shəmpi`o

---

championship

шампионат

shəmpio`na

---

cleats

бутонки

bu`tonk

---

club

стик

sti

---

competition

състезание

səste`zani

---

course

курс

kur

---

court

корт

kor

---

cricket

крикет

`krike

---

cup

купа

`kup

---

curling

кърлинг

`kʌrlin

---

cycling

колоездене

kolo`ezden

---

darts

дартс

dart

---

defense

защита

zə`shtit

---

diving

гмуркане

`gmurkən

---

dodgeball

доджбол

`dodzhbo

---

driver

шофьор

sho`fyo

---

equestrian

конен

`kone

---

event

събитие

sə`biti

---

fan

фен

fe

---

fencing

фехтовка

fek`tovk

---

field

поле

po`l

figure skating

фигурно пързаляне

`figurno pər`zalyən

fishing

риболов

ribo`lo

football

футбол

`futbo

game

игра

ig`r

gear

екипировка

ekipi`rovk

goal

гол

go

golf

голф

gol

golf club

стик за голф

stik za gol

---

gym

фитнес център

`fitness `tzentə

---

gymnastics

гимнастика

gim`nastik

---

halftime

полувреме

polu`vrem

---

helmet

каска

`kask

---

hockey

хокей

`hoke

---

horse racing

конно надбягване

`konno nəd`byagvən

---

hunting

лов

lo

---

ice skating

кънки на лед

`kʌnki na le

---

inning

ининг

`inin

---

jockey

жокей

zho`ke

---

judo

джудо

`dzhud

---

karate

карате

kə`rat

---

kayaking

каяк

kə`ya

---

kickball

кикбол

`kikbo

---

lacrosse

лакрос

lək`ro

---

league

лига

`lig

---

martial arts

бойни изкуства

`boyni iz`kustv

---

mat

тепих

te`pi

---

match

мач

mac

---

medal

медал

me`da

---

net

мрежа

`mrezh

---

offense

нападение

napə`deni

Olympic Games

Олимпийски игри

olim`piyski ig`r

---

pentathlon

петобой

peto`bo

---

pitch

игрище

ig`risht

---

play

игра

ig`r

---

player

играч

ig`rac

---

polo

поло

`pol

---

pool

билярд

bi`lyar

---

pool cue

щека за билярд

`shtekə za bi`lyar

---

professional

професионалист

profesionə`lis

---

puck
шайба
`shayb

---

quarter
четвъртина
chetvər`tin

---

race
състезание
səste`zani

---

race car
състезателна кола
səste`zatelnə ko`l

---

racket
ракета
rə`ket

---

record
рекорд
re`kor

---

referee
съдия
sədi`y

---

relay
щафета
shtə`fet

---

riding

езда

ez`d

---

ring

ринг

rin

---

rink

пързалка (за хокей, кънки)

pər`zalkə (za `hokey, `kʌnki

---

rowing

гребане

`grebən

---

rugby

ръгби

`rʌgb

---

running

тичане

`tichən

---

saddle

седло

sed`l

---

sailing

плаване

`plavən

---

score

резултат

rezul`ta

---

shuffleboard

вид хазартна игра

vid hə`zartnə ig`r

---

shuttle cock

перце

per`tz

---

skates

кънки

`kənk

---

skating

пързаляне

pər`zalk

---

skiing

ски

sk

---

skis

ски

sk

---

soccer

футбол

`futbo

---

softball

софтбол

`softbo

---

spectators

зрители

`zritel

---

sport

спорт

spor

---

sportsmanship

спортсменство

sports`menstv

---

squash

скуош

sku`os

---

stadium

стадион

stədi`o

---

surf

сърф

sʌr

---

surfboard

сърф

sʌr

---

swimming

плуване

`pluvən

---

table tennis/ping pong

тенис на маса/пинг понг

`tenis na `masə/ping pon

---

tag

гоненица

`gonenitz

---

team

отбор

ot`bo

---

tennis

тенис

`teni

---

tetherball

тетърбол

`tetərbo

---

throw

хвърляне

`hvʌrlyan

---

track

писта

`psit

---

track and field

лека атлетика

`lekə ət`letik

---

volleyball

волейбол

`voleybo

---

water skiing

водни ски

`vodni sk

---

weight lifting

вдигане на тежести

`vdigəne na `tezhest

---

whistle

свирка

`svirk

---

win

победа

po`bed

---

windsurfing

уиндсърфинг

`uindsərfin

---

winner

победител

pobe`dite

---

wrestling
борба
bor`b

Related Verbs

to catch
хващам
`hvashtə

---

to cheat
мамя
`mamy

---

to compete
състезавам се
səste`zavəm s

---

to dribble
дриблирам
drib`lirə

---

to go
вървя
vər`vy

---

to hit
удрям
`udrya

---

to jump

скачам

`skachə

to kick

ритам

`ritə

to knock out

нокаутирам

nokəu`tirə

to lose

губя

`guby

to play

играя

ig`ray

to race

състезавам се

səste`zavəm s

to run

тичам

`tichə

to score

отбелязвам

otbe`lyazvə

to win

печеля

pe`chely

Sports are an important part of our culture and have been throughout all history. Men specifically, are drawn to **sports** because of their competitive nature. From the time they are four or five years old, little boys are playing **sports** such as **baseball, soccer**, and **basketball**. They grow up to be men and their competitive nature grows with them. Contact **sports**, such as American **football, dodgeball, boxing, hockey**, and **wrestling** are popular among men because of their competitiveness. Women also enjoy **sports**, but usually prefer **sports** with less contact, such as **tennis, figure skating, gymnastics**, and **swimming**. In recent years, women are participating in more contact **sports** than ever before. Even retirees enjoy playing **sports, games** such as **golf** and **shuffleboard** are popular among the older crowd. Not only do people enjoy playing **sports**, they love to watch **sports** as well. Wherever you travel, you are sure to see a **fan** or two dressed in their favorite **team** colors. **Sports fan** merchandise is a huge industry. **Sports fans** spend a lot of money every year to buy **tickets** to events to cheer on their **team**. The most popular sporting **event** in the world is the **Olympic Games**. Most **athletes** dream of becoming an **Olympic medalist**. Although, there are some similarities, the **event** has changed quite a bit over the years. The **Olympics** have a rich history and began in Greece. **Sports** played an important role in Greek culture; playing a part in religious festivals as well as used as training for the Greek military. The **Olympics** began as a festival of **sporting events** that was very popular among the people; there were over 30 thousand **spectators** in attendance. The

Greeks competed in **track and field events**, such as **running, javelin, long jump, discus,** just to name a few. They also **wrestled** and had **boxing matches**. The most popular event was the **pentathlon**, which included five **events**: the **long jump, javelin, discus**, a foot **race**, and **boxing**. The **Olympic Games** and the **sports** involved have changed since that first **event**. Today's **Olympic Games** are held in a different city each year. Over 10 thousand **athletes** compete in over 300 **events**! Some of the sports in the Modern **Olympic Games** are **archery, diving, basketball, cycling, volleyball, boxing**, and the modern **pentathlon** which includes **fencing, swimming,** show jumping**(equestrian)**, pistol **shooting**, and a cross country **run.**

Спортовете са важна част от нашата култура и са били такива през цялата история. Особено мъжете са привличани от **спорта** поради състезателната си природа. От времето, когато са на четири или пет малките момчета играят **спортове**, като **бейзбол, футбол** и **баскетбол**. Те порастват мъже и тяхната състезателна природа пораства с тях. Контактните **спортове**, като американски **футбол, доджбол, бокс, хокей** и **борба,** са популярни сред мъжете поради техния състезателен характер. Жените също обичат **спортовете**, но обикновено предпочитат **спортове** с по-малко контакт, като **тенис, фигурно пързаляне, гимнастика** и **плуване**. През последните години жените участват в повече контактни **спортове** от когато и да било преди. Дори пенсионерите обичат да играят **спортове –** игри като **голф** и **хазартни игри** са популярни сред по-старата част от хората. Хората не само обичат да играят **спортове**, те обичат и да гледат **спортове**. Когато пътувате, със сигурност ще видите един или два **фена,**

облечени в цветовете на любимите си отбори. Стоките за **фенове на спорта** са огромна индустрия. **Феновете на спорта** харчат много пари всяка година, за да си купят **билети** за събития, за да подкрепят своя **отбор**. Най-популярното спортно **събитие** в света са **Олимпийските игри**. Повечето **атлети** си мечтаят да станат **олимпийски медалисти**. Въпреки че има някои прилики, **събитието** се е променило доста през годините. **Олимпийските игри** имат богата история и възникват в Гърция. **Спортовете** са играли важна роля в гръцката култура, участвайки в религиозните фестивали и са били използвани за гръцката армия. **Олимпийските игри** започнали като фестивал на **спортни събития**, който бил много популярен сред хората – присъствали над 30 хиляди **зрители**. Гърците се състезавали в **лекоатлетически събития**, като **тичане, хвърляне на копие, дълъг скок, хвърляне на диск** и други. Освен това те упражнявали **борба** и **боксови мачове**. Най-популярното събитие бил **петобоят**, който включвал пет **събития: дълъг скок, хвърляне на копие, хвърляне на диск, надбягване** и **бокс**. **Олимпийските игри** и включените **спортове** са се променили от първото такова събитие. Днешните **Олимпийски игри** се провеждат в различен град всеки път. Над 10 хиляди **атлета** се състезават в над 300 **събития**! Някои от спортовете в модерните **Олимпийски игри** са **стрелба с лък, гмуркане, баскетбол, колоездене, волейбол, бокс** и модерният петобой, който включва **фехтовка, плуване,** прескачане на препятствия **(конни), стреляне** с пистолет и **бягане** в пресечна местност.

11) Food

apple
ябълка
`yabəlk

---

bacon
бекон
be`ko

---

bagel
кравайче
krə`vaych

---

banana
банан
bə`na

---

beans
боб
bo

---

beef
говеждо
go`vezhd

---

bread
хляб
hlya

---

broccoli
броколи
`brokol

---

brownie
брауни
`braun

---

cake
торта
`tort

---

candy
бонбон
bon`bo

---

carrot
морков
`morko

---

celery
целина
`tzelin

---

cheese
сирене
`siren

---

cheesecake
чийзкейк
`chiyzkey

chicken

пиле

`pil`

chocolate

шоколад

shoko`la

cinnamon

канела

kə`nel

cookie

бисквита

bis`kvit

crackers

крекери

`kreker

dip

сос

so

eggplant

патладжан

pətlə`dzha

fig

смокиня

smo`kiny

fish

риба

`rib

fruit

плод

plo

garlic

чесън

`chesə

ginger

джинджифил

dzhindzhi`fi

ham

шунка

`shunk

herbs

подправки

pod`pravk

honey

мед

me

ice cream

сладолед

sladо`le

jelly/jam
желе / конфитюр
zhe`le/konfi`tyu

ketchup
кетчуп
`ketchu

lemon
лимон
li`mo

lettuce
маруля
mə`ruly

mahi mahi
Махи Махи
`mahi `mah

mango
манго
`mang

mayonnaise
майонеза
məyo`nez

meat
месо
me`s

melon

пъпеш

`pʌpes`

milk

мляко

mlyak

mustard

горчица

gor`chitz

noodles

юфка

yuf`k

nuts

ядки

`yatk`

oats

овес

o`ve

olive

маслина

məs`lin

orange

портокал

porto`ka

pasta
макаронени изделия
məkə`roneni iz`deliy

pastry
сладкиши
sləd`kish

pepper
чушка
`chushk

pork
свинско
`svinsk

potato
картоф
kər`to

pumpkin
тиква
`tikv

raisin
стафида
stə`fid

sage
градински чай
grə`dinski cha

salad

салата

sə`lat

---

salmon

сьомга

`syomg

---

sandwich

сандвич

`sandvic

---

sausage

наденица

`nadenitz

---

soup

супа

`sup

---

squash

тиква

`tikv

---

steak

пържола

pər`zhol

---

strawberry

ягода

`yagod

---

sugar

захар

`zahə`

tea

чай

cha

toast

препечена филия

pre`pechenə fi`liy

tomato

домат

do`ma

vinegar

оцет

o`tze

vegetables

зеленчуци

zelen`chutz

water

вода

vo`d

wheat

пшеница

pshe`nitz

yogurt

кисело мляко

`kiselo `mlyak

Restaurants and Cafes

a la carte

алакарт

ələ`kar

a la mode

с топка сладолед

s `topkə slədo`le

appetizer

предястие

pred`yasti

bar

бар

ba

beverage

напитка

nə`pitk

bill

сметка

`smetk

bistro
бистро
bis`tr

---

boiled
варен
və`re

---

bowl
купа
`kup

---

braised
запържен
zə`pərzhe

---

breakfast
закуска
zə`kusk

---

brunch
късна закуска
`kʌsnə zə`kusk

---

cafe/cafeteria
кафене
kə`fen

---

cashier
касиер
kəsi`e

---

chair

стол

sto

charge

цена

tze`n

check

чек

che

chef

главен готвач

`glaven got`vac

coffee

кафе

kə`f

coffee shop

кафене

kəfe`n

condiments

подправки

pod`pravk

cook

готвач

got`vac

courses
ястия
`yastiy

---

credit card
кредитна карта
`kreditnə `kart

---

cup
чаша
`chash

---

cutlery
прибори
`pribor

---

deli/delicatessen
деликатеси
delikə`tes

---

dessert
десерт
de`ser

---

dine
вечеря
ve`chery

---

diner
крайпътен ресторант
krəy`pəten resto`ran

---

dinner

вечеря

ve`chery

dish

ястие

`yasti

dishwasher

мияч на чинии

`miyach nə `chini

doggie bag

торбичка за остатъци от храна

tor`bichkə zə os`tatətzi ot hrə`n

drink

питие

piti`

entree

предястие

pred`yasti

food

храна

hrə`n

fork

вилица

`vilitz

glass

чаша

`chash

---

gourmet

гурме

gur`m

---

hor d'oeuvre

ордьовър

or`dyovə

---

host/hostess

домакин/домакиня

domə`kin/ domə`kiny

---

knife

нож

noz

---

lunch

обяд

o`bya

---

maitre d'

оберкелнер

`ober`kelne

---

manager

мениджър

`menidzhə

---

menu
меню
me`ny

mug
чаша
`chash

napkin
салфетка
səl`fetk

order
поръчка
po`rəchk

party
парти
`part

plate
чиния
chi`niy

platter
поднос
pod`no

reservation
резервация
rezer`vatziy

restaurant

ресторант

resto`ran

---

saucer

чинийка за кафе

`chiniykə za kə`f

---

server

сервитьор

servi`tyo

---

side order

гарнитура

gərni`tur

---

silverware

сребърни прибори

`srebərni `pribor

---

special

специалитет

spetziəli`te

---

spoon

лъжица

lə`zhitz

---

starters

предястия

pred`yastiy

---

supper

вечеря

ve`chery

table

маса

`mas

tax

данък

`danə

tip

бакшиш

bak`shis

to go

за вкъщи

zə `vkəsht

utensils

прибори

`pribor

waiter/waitress

сервитьор/сервитьорка

servi`tyor/ servi`tyork

Related Verbs

to bake

пека

pe`k

to be hungry

гладен съм

`gladen sə

to cook

готвя

`gotvy

to cut

режа

`rezh

to drink

пия

`piy

to eat

ям

ya

to eat out

ям навън

yam na`və

to feed

храня

`hrany

---

to grow

отглеждам

ot`glezhdə

---

to have breakfast

закусвам

zə`kusvə

---

to have lunch

обядвам

o`byadvə

---

to have dinner

вечерям

ve`cheryə

---

to make

правя

`pravy

---

to order

поръчвам

po`rəchvə

---

to pay

плащам

`plashtə

---

to prepare

приготвям

pri`gotvyə

---

to request

искам

`iskə

---

to reserve

резервирам

rezer`virə

---

to serve

сервирам

ser`virə

---

to set the table

слагам масата

`slagəm `masət

---

to taste

опитвам

o`pitvə

John and Mary have been dating for quite some time now. Next week is their two year anniversary and John wants to make it really special. Mary really enjoys a nice **steak dinner** out, so John is going to make **reservations** at her favorite **restaurant**. She will be so surprised because they haven't eaten there in a while and she just loves their **salad** and **bread**. John calls and speaks to the **manager** ahead of time to set up the **reservation**. Finally, the day arrives and John picks Mary up at her home. She still doesn't know where they are going, but is excited for the surprise. "Where are we going? Mary asked. "I told you, it's a surprise!" said John. So Mary begins trying to guess where their surprise destination is. "Is it our favorite **diner**? I love the laid back atmosphere and the **waitress** is so nice." "Is it the **coffee shop** on the corner? You know how much I love **coffee**." They arrive at the **restaurant** and she squeals with delight at the thought of the **cheesecake** that they serve for **dessert** . The **host** greets them at the door and promptly seats them at their favorite **table** near the **bar**. It is a quiet little corner of the **restaurant**. The server greets them, lays a **napkin** and **silverware** on their **table**, and then takes their **drink order**. She offers them an **appetizer** while they wait. When the **server** returns, she begins to tell the couple about the daily **specials**. "We'll have two of your best steak **dinners**." John said, "Nothing but the best for my girl!" They are really enjoying their **gourmet meal** and the conversation is great, as always. I think we should have **dessert** for this special night. John tells the **server** that they would like a **brownie a la mode t**o share. The server brings the delicious brownie on a **plate** with two **spoons**. John and Mary both look at the **dessert** and decide they do not have room to eat it. "I think we will need that **to-go**," said Mary. While waiting for the server to pack up their **doggie bag**, John surprised Mary by getting down on his knee to propose! The whole **restaurant** was clapping; even the **dishwasher** and **cooks** came out to congratulate the couple. What a wonderful second anniversary this turned out to be for the happy couple. Now, every year on their anniversary, they **dine** at their favorite **restaurant** to celebrate such a wonderful evening.

Джон и Мери се срещат от известно време. Следващата седмица е тяхната втора годишнина и Джон иска да я направи наистина специална. Мери много обича да **вечеря** навън, затова Джон ще направи **резервация** в любимия ѝ **ресторант**. Тя ще бъде толкова изненадана, защото те не са се хранили там отдавна, а тя много обича тяхната **салата** и **хляб**. Джон се обажда и говори с **мениджъра** предварително, за да уреди **резервацията**. Накрая денят пристига и Джон взима Мери от дома ѝ. Тя не знае къде отиват, но се вълнува заради изненадата. „Къде отиваме?", пита Мери. „Казах ти, това е изненада!", казва Джон. Мери започва да се опитва да познае къде ще бъде изненадата. „Да не би да е любимият ни **крайпътен ресторант**? Обичам спокойната атмосфера и **сервитьорката** е толкова мила." „Да не би да е **кафенето** на ъгъла? Знаеш колко много обичам **кафе**." Те пристигат в **ресторанта** и тя изпищява от задоволство при мисълта за **чийзкейка**, който сервират за **десерт**. **Домакинът** ги посреща на вратата и ги настанява на любимата им **маса** до **бара**. Това е малка, тиха част на **ресторанта**. Сервитьорката ги поздравява, поставя **салфетка** и **сребърни прибори** на **масата** им и взима **поръчката им за питиета**. Тя има предлага **предястие** докато чакат. Когато **сервитьорката** се връща, им казва за дневните **специалитети**. „Ще вземем две от най-добрите ви пържоли за **вечеря**.", казва Джон. „Само най-доброто за моето момиче!" Те наистина се наслаждават на своята **гурме храна**, а разговорът е страхотен, както винаги. Мисля, че трябва да хапнем **десерт** в тази специална нощ. Джон казва на **сервитьорката**, че биха искали едно **брауни с топка сладолед** за двамата. Сервитьорката носи вкусното брауни в **чиния** с две **лъжици**. Джон и Мери гледат **десерта** и решават, че нямат място да го ядат. „Смятам, че трябва да вземем това **за вкъщи**.", казва Мери. Докато чакат сервитьорката да опакова **торбичката им за вкъщи**, Джон изненадва Мери, като пада на колене и й предлага! Целият **ресторант** ръкопляска. Дори и **миячът на чинии** и **готвачите** излизат, за да поздравят двойката. Каква чудесна втора годишнина се оказа тази за щастливата двойка. Сега всяка година на своята годишнина, те **вечерят** в любимия си **ресторант** и празнуват страхотна вечер.

12) Shopping

bags
торби
tor`b

---

bakery
пекарница
pe`karnitz

---

barcode
баркод
`barko

---

basket
кошница
`koshnitz

---

bookstore
книжарница
kni`zharnitz

---

boutique
бутик
bu`ti

---

browse
търся
`tʌrsy

---

buggy/shopping cart

пазарска количка

pə`zarskə ko`lichk

---

butcher

касапин

kə`sapi

---

buy

купувам

ku`puvə

---

cash

пари

pə`r

---

cashier

касиер

kəsi`e

---

change

ресто

`rest

---

changing room

пробна

`probn

---

cheap

евтин

`evti

---

check

чек

chec

---

clearance

разпродажба

rəzpro`dazhb

---

coin

монета

mo`net

---

convenience store

денонощен магазин

deno`noshten məgə`zi

---

counter

щанд

shtan

---

credit card

кредитна карта

`kreditnə `kart

---

customers

клиенти

kli`ent

---

debit card

дебитна карта

`debitnə `kart

---

delivery

доставка

dos`tavk

---

department store

универсален магазин

univer`salen məgə`zi

---

discount

отстъпка

ot`stəpk

---

discount store

дисконтен магазин

dis`konten məgə`zi

---

drugstore/pharmacy

аптека

əp`tek

---

electronic store

магазин за електроника

məgə`zin za elek`tronik

---

escalator

ескалатор

eskə`lato

---

expensive

скъп

skʌ

---

flea market

битпазар

`bitpə`za

---

florist

цветар

tzve`ta

---

grocery store

хранителен магазин

hrə`nitelen məgə`zi

---

hardware

железария

zhelezə`riy

---

jeweler

бижутер

bizhu`te

---

mall

мол

mo

---

market

пазар

pə`za

---

meat department

отдел за месо

ot`del za me`s

---

music store

музикален магазин

muzi`kalen məgə`zi

---

offer

оферта

o`fert

---

pet store

магазин за животни

məgə`zin za zhi`votn

---

purchase

покупка

`danə

---

purse

портмоне

po`kupk

---

rack

рафт

raf

---

receipt

касова бележка

`kasovə be`lezhk

---

return

връщам

`vrʌshtə

---

sale
разпродажба
rəzpro`dazhb

sales person
продавач
prodə`vac

scale
кантар
kən`ta

size
размер
rəz`me

shelf/shelves
рафт/рафтове
raft/`raftov

shoe store
магазин за обувки
məgə`zin za o`buvk

shop
магазин
məgə`zi

shopping center
търговски център
`tərgovski `tzentə

store

магазин

məgə`zi

---

supermarket

супермаркет

`super`marke

---

tailor

шивач

shi`vac

---

till

касов апарат

`kasov əpə`ra

---

toy store

магазин за играчки

məgə`zin za ig`rachk

---

wallet

портфейл

port`fey

---

wholesale

търговия на едро

tərgo`viya na `edr

Related Verbs

to buy

купувам

ku`puvə

---

to charge

таксувам

tək`suvə

---

to choose

избирам

iz`birə

---

to exchange

разменям

raz`menyə

---

to go shopping

пазарувам

pəzə`ruvə

---

to owe

притежавам

prite`zhavə

---

to pay

плащам

`plashtə

---

to prefer

предпочитам

pretpoˋchitə

---

to return

връщам

ˋvrəshtə

---

to save

спестявам

spesˋtyavə

---

to sell

продавам

proˋdavə

---

to shop

пазарувам

pəzəˋruvə

---

to spend

харча

ˋharch

---

to try on

пробвам

ˋprobvə

---

to want

искам

ˋiskə

It was just a few weeks until Christmas and Mark needed to **purchase** a gift for his wife. He didn't know what he was going to get for her. First, he went to the **bookstore**, she loved to read books. He checked the **shelves** to see if he could find something she had not read before, but he had no luck with that. Then he decided to visit her favorite clothing **boutique**. The **salesperson** was very friendly and helpful as he shopped. She knew his wife and was able to help him with **sizes**. He **browsed** the **racks** for just the right gift, but he did not find anything he thought she would like. Besides, everything was so **expensive!** Next, he went to the **shoe store**. He looked around and just couldn't decide what to get for her, so he left that **store**. He resisted going to the **hardware store**, that is his favorite. He thought to himself, "I have to remember, I am **shopping** for my wife, not me!" He finally decided to go to the **mall**. There are plenty of **shops** there! As he walked through the **mall**, he was getting discouraged; he passed a couple of **department stores**, a **music store** and a **toy store**, but nothing seemed right. Finally, he came upon a **jeweler.** His wife loves jewelry. He approached the **counter** and began telling the **salesman** about his wife and the type of jewelry she wears. He was so excited to learn that the ring he picked out was on **sale**. The **salesman** told him the total and Mark reached for his **wallet** to get the **cash**. He asked the salesman, "Does that **price** include **tax**?" "Yes, of course", replied the **salesman**. Mark realized he didn't have enough **cash**, so he paid with his **credit card**. The salesman thanked him and gave him the ring and **receipt**. Mark was so pleased to have found a gift for his wife. He stopped by the **florist** on the way home to surprise her with some flowers. As he was leaving the **florist**, his wife called and asked him to stop by the **grocery store** on his way home. Mark decided he could get what he needed from the **convenience store**, so he stopped there, and then headed home to his wife. She was so surprised that he bought her flowers. She had a little surprise for him as well; she had stopped at the **bakery** on her way home from work. He thanked her for her thoughtful surprise. How lucky he felt to be in such a giving marriage!

Оставаха само няколко седмици до Коледа и Марк трябваше да **купи** подарък за съпругата си. Той не знаеше какво ще ѝ вземе. Първо отиде до **книжарницата** – тя обичаше да чете книги. Той провери **рафтовете**, за да види дали ще може да намери нещо, което тя не е чела, но нямаше късмет. След това реши да посети любимия ѝ **бутик** за дрехи. **Продавачката** беше много любезна и отзивчива докато той пазаруваше. Тя познаваше съпругата му и можеше да му помогне с **размерите**. Тя **претърси рафтовете** за точния подарък, но не откри нищо, което смяташе, че ще ѝ хареса. Освен това всичко беше толкова **скъпо**! След това той отиде в **магазина за обувки**. Огледа се и просто не можа да реши какво да ѝ купи, затова си тръгна от **магазина**. Той устоя на това да отиде в **железарията,** любимо негово място. Помисли си: „Трябва да помня, че пазарувам за съпругата си, не за себе си!" Накрая реши да отиде в **мола**. Там има много **магазини**! Докато се разхождаше в **мола,** той се обезкуражи; мина покрай няколко **универсални магазина, музикален магазин** и **магазин за играчки**, но нищо не изглеждаше подходящо. Накрая той се натъкна на **бижутер**. Съпругата му обича бижута. Той се доближи до **щанда** и започна да разказва на **продавача** за съпругата му и вида бижута, които тя носи. Той беше много развълнуван да научи, че пръстенът, който избра, беше на

разпродажба. Продавачът му каза каква е цената и Марк се бръкна за **портфейла** си, за да вземе **пари**. Той попита продавача: „Тази **цена** включва ли **данъка**?" „Да, разбира се", отговори **продавачът**. Марк осъзна, че нямаше достатъчно **пари в брой**, затова плати с **кредитна карта**. Продавачът му благодари и му даде пръстена и **касовата бележка**. Марк беше толкова доволен, че е открил подарък за съпругата си. Той спря при **цветарския магазин** на път за вкъщи, за да я изненада с цветя. Когато излизаше от **цветарския магазин**, съпругата му се обади и го помоли да мине през **хранителния магазин,** когато се прибира. Марк реши, че може да вземе каквото му трябва от **денонощния магазин**, затова спря там и след това се запъти към къщи при жена си. Тя беше толкова изненадана, че ѝ е купил цветя. И тя имаше малка изненада за него; беше се отбила през **пекарницата** на път за вкъщи от работа. Той ѝ благодари за замислената изненада. Колко щастлив се почувства, че има толкова щедър брак!

13) At the Bank

account

сметка

`smetk

APR/Annual Percentage Rate

ГПР/ Годишен процент на разходите

go`dishen pro`tzent nə `razhodit

ATM/Automatic Teller Machine

банкомат

bənko`ma

---

balance

баланс

bə`lan

---

bank

банка

`bank

---

bank charges

банкови такси

`bankovi `taks

---

bank draft

банково платежно нареждане

`bankovo plə`tezhno nə`rezhdən

---

bank rate

обменен курс

ob`menen kur

---

bank statement

банково извлечение

`bankovo izvle`cheni

---

borrower

кредитополучател

kreditopolu`chate

---

bounced check

чек, който не може да бъде изплатен

chek `koyto ne `mozhe da `bəde izplə`te

---

cardholder

картодържател

kərtodər`zhate

---

cash

пари в брой

pa`ri v bro

---

cashback

кешбек

`keshbe

---

check

чек

che

---

checkbook
чекова книжка
`chekova `knizhk

checking account
разплащателна сметка
rəzplə`shtatelnə `smetk

collateral
допълнителна гаранция
dopəl`nitelnə gə`ranciy

commission
комисионна
komisi`onn

credit
кредит
`kredi

credit card
кредитна карта
`kreditnə `kart

credit limit
кредитен лимит
`krediten `limi

credit rating
кредитен рейтинг
`krediten `reytin

currency

валута

və`lut

---

debt

дълг

dʌl

---

debit

дебит

`debi

---

debit card

дебитна карта

`debitnə `kart

---

deposit

депозит

de`pozi

---

direct debit

директен дебит

di`rekten `debi

---

direct deposit

директен депозит

di`rekten de`pozi

---

expense

разход

`razho

---

fees
такси
`taks

---

foreign exchange rate
валутен курс
və`luten kur

---

insurance
застраховка
zəstrə`hovk

---

interest
лихва
`lihv

Internet banking
интернет банкиране
inter`net bən`kiran

---

loan
заем
`zae

---

money
пари
pə`r

---

money market
паричен пазар
pə`richen pə`za

---

mortgage

ипотека

ipo`tek

NSF/Insufficient Funds

недостатъчна наличност

nedos`tatəchnə nə`lichnos

---

online banking

онлайн банкиране

`onlayn bən`kirən

---

overdraft

овърдрафт

`ovər`draf

---

payee

бенефициент

benefitzi`en

---

pin number

ПИН код

`pinko

---

register

регистър

re`gistə

---

savings account

спестовна сметка

spes`tovnə `smetk

---

statement
извлечение
izvle`cheni

tax
данък
`danə

telebanking
телебанкиране
telebən`kirən

teller
касиер
kasi`e

transaction
транзакция
trənz`akciy

traveler's check
пътнически чек
`pətnicheski che

vault
трезор
tre`zo

withdraw
тегля
`tegly

Related Verbs

to borrow

заемам

zə`emə

---

to cash

осребрявам

osreb`ryavə

---

to charge

таксувам

taksu`və

---

to deposit

депозирам

depo`zirə

---

to endorse

подписвам се като поръчител

pod`pisvəm se kə`to porə`chite

---

to enter

вписвам

`vpisvə

---

to hold

държа

dər`zh

---

to insure

обезпечавам

obezpe`chavə

---

to lend

заемам

zə`emə

---

to open an account

откривам си сметка

ot`krivəm si `smetk

---

to pay

плащам

`plashtə

---

to save

спестявам

spes`tyavə

---

to spend

харча

`harch

---

to transfer money

прехвърлям пари

pre`hvərlyəm pə`r

---

to withdraw

тегля

`tegly

If you have a job, you will probably want to open a **bank account**. The two most popular **accounts** available are **checking account** and **savings account. Banks** also have many other **account** options, including **credit** lines, **money market accounts, mortgages**, etc. A **checking account** is good for your day-to-day purchases and paying your bills. You usually receive a **check card,** which works similar to a **credit card** for purchases, and a **checkbook** when you open a **checking account**. Your **check card** works like a **credit card**, however it **withdraws** money directly from your **account**. **Checks** are good for paying friends and family, bills, or anytime you have to mail a payment to someone. Most merchant's accept **checks** or **check cards** for payment, so you should not have a problem with everyday purchases with your **checking account**. You can also use your **debit card** to **withdraw cash** from **ATMs**; you will need to set up a **pin number** for **ATM transactions**. Make sure you keep track of your purchases and **withdrawals** using the **check register** because you don't want to be hit with **NSF fees**. As long as you **deposit** more **money** that you take out, you will be safe from **bank fees**. Many **banks** offer **Online Bill Pay**, making it very convenient for you to pay your bills from the comfort of your home, without ever needing to purchase a stamp. Another popular **bank account** is called a **savings account**. A **savings account** is great for long term planning. **Savings accounts** pay you **interest** on the **money** in your **account**. Different **banks** offer different **interest** rates based upon your savings habits and *balance.* This is the **account** you want to put money into and only take it out in case of emergency. **Checking** and **savings accounts** work well together and are the most common types of **bank accounts** available. Many savings accounts offer **overdraft** protection for your **checking account**. If you mess up and **withdraw** too much **money**, your **savings account** funds will step in and keep you from being charged **overdraft fees**. **Banks** are a safe way to save and manage your money. There are many safeguards in place to protect your **accounts**. With so many features, such as **online bill pay, telephone banking,** and **direct deposit,** the smart and efficient way to manage your money is with a **bank account**.

Ако имате работа, може би ще искате да си откриете **банкова сметка**. Двете най-популярни **сметки** са **разплащателна сметка** и **спестовна сметка**. Банките имат и много други опции за **сметки**, включително **кредитни** линии, **сметки за паричния пазар, ипотеки** и др. **Разплащателната сметка** е подходяща за ежедневните ви покупки и плащане на сметки. Вие обикновено получавате **чекова карта**, която работи подобно на **кредитна карта** за покупки и **чекова книжка**, когато си откривате **разплащателна сметка**. Вашата **чекова карта** работи като **кредитна карта**, но **тегли** пари директно от вашата **сметка**. **Чековете** са добри за плащане на приятели и роднини, сметки или всеки път, когато трябва да изпратите плащане на някого. Повечето търговци приемат **чекове** или **чекови карти** за плащане, затова не би трябвало да имате проблем с ежедневните си покупки с **чековата си сметка**. Можете да използвате и **дебитна карта**, за да **теглите пари в брой** от **банкомати**; трябва да имате **ПИН код** за **транзакции на банкомат**. Уверете се, че следите покупките и **тегленията** си, като използвате **чековия регистър**, защото не искате да ви се наложат такси за **недостатъчна наличност**. Докато **депозирате** повече пари, отколкото теглите, няма да ви се налагат **банкови такси**. Много **банки** предлагат **онлайн**

плащане на сметки, което е много удобно за вас да плащате сметките си от удобството на своя дом, без дори да се налага да купувате марка. Друга популярна **банкова сметка** се нарича **спестовна сметка**. Спестовната сметка е страхотна за дългосрочно планиране. **Спестовните сметки** плащат **лихва** на **парите** във вашата **сметка**. Различните **банки** предлагат различни **лихви** въз основа на вашите навици за спестяване и *баланс*. Това е **сметката**, в която искате да слагате пари и да ги теглите само при спешни случаи. **Разплащателните** и **спестовни сметки** работят добре заедно и са най-често срещаните видове **сметки**. Много спестовни сметки предлагат **овърдрафт** защита за вашата **разплащателна сметка**. Ако се объркате и **изтеглите** прекалено много **пари**, средствата от вашата **спестовна сметка** ще се намесят и ще ви предпазят от **такси за овърдрафт**. **Банките** са безопасен начин да пестите и управлявате парите си. Има много гаранции, които да защитават вашите **сметки**. С толкова много функции, като **онлайн плащане на сметки**, **телефонно банкиране** и **директни депозити**, умният и ефективен начин да управлявате парите си е с **банкова сметка**.

14) Holidays

balloons
балони
bə`lon

---

calendar
календар
kəlen`da

---

celebrate
празнувам
prəz`nuvə

---

celebration
празненство
prəznens`tv

---

commemorating
честване
`chestvən

---

decorations
украси
uk`ras

---

family
семейство
se`meystv

---

feast

празник

`prazni

federal

федерален

fede`rale

festivities

празненства

prəznens`tv

fireworks

фойерверки

`foyer`verk

first

първи

`pʌrv

friends

приятели

pri`yatel

games

игри

ig`r

gifts

подаръци

po`darətz

heroes
герои
ge`ro

holiday
празник
`prazni

honor
чест
ches

national
национален
natzio`nale

parade
парад
pə`ra

party
парти
`part

picnics
пикници
`piknitz

remember
спомням си
`spomnyam s

resolution

решение

re`sheni

---

traditions

традиции

trə`ditzi

American Holidays in calendar order:

New Year's Day

Нова година

`novə go`din

Martin Luther King Jr. Day

Ден на Мартин Лутър Кинг Младши

den na `martin `lutər king `mladsh

Groundhog Day

Ден на мармота

den na mər`mot

Valentine's Day

Свети Валентин

sve`ti vəlen`ti

St. Patrick's Day

Ден на Свети Патрик

den na sve`ti `patri

Easter
Великден
ve`likde

April Fool's Day
Ден на шегата
den na she`gat

Earth Day
Ден на земята
den na ze`myat

Mother's Day
Ден на майката
den na `maykət

Memorial Day
Ден на загиналите във войните
den na zə`ginəlite vəv voy`nit

Father's Day
Ден на бащата
den na bə`shtat

Flag Day
Ден на националния флаг
den na natzio`naliniya fla

Independence Day/July 4th
Ден на независимостта/4 юли
den na nezəvisimost`t

Labor Day

Ден на труда

den na tru`d

Columbus Day

Ден на Колумб

den na ko`lum

Halloween

Хелоуин

`heloui

Veteran's Day

Ден на ветераните

den na vete`ranit

Election Day

Изборен ден

`izboren de

Thanksgiving Day

Ден на благодарността

den na blagodərnost`t

Christmas

Коледа

`koled

Hanukkah

Ханука

`hanuk

New Year's Eve
Нова година
`novə go`din

Related Verbs

to celebrate
празнувам
prəz`nuvə

---

to cherish
грижа се за
`grizhə se z

---

to commemorate
отбелязвам
otbe`lyazvə

---

to cook
готвя
`gotvy

---

to give
давам
`davə

---

to go to
отивам на
o`tivəm n

---

to honor

почитам

po`chitə

to observe

чествам

`chestvə

to party

празнувам

prəz`nuvə

to play

играя

ig`ray

to recognize

признавам

priz`navə

to remember

спомням си

`spomnyam s

to visit

посещавам

pose`shtavə

Many cultures and backgrounds are represented in America. With such diversity, Americans **celebrate** many **holidays** throughout the year. There are so many **holidays** on the **calendar**, there is always something to **celebrate**. In

January, **New Year's Day** is a big **celebration**, but the real celebrating comes the night before; there are **fireworks** and **parties** that are broadcast all over the world. In February, we celebrate **Valentine's Day**. It is a day that most couples express their love and affection for each other with cards and gifts. In March, we celebrate **St. Patrick's Day**. Many people wear green items and celebrate Irish heritage. **Easter** is usually celebrated in April. It is a Christian **holiday**, but has also become a secular **holiday** celebrating the beginning of springtime. One of the most cherished **holidays** in America is **Mother's Day**. We honor and remember our mothers and grandmothers on this day; showering them with cards, gifts, and affection. Another big **holiday** in May is **Memorial Day**; originally declared as a day to remember our fallen **heroes** of the various branches of the United States military. It is now seen as the unofficial start of summertime and is celebrated with **picnics** and time with **family**. In June, we **celebrate Father's Day**, while it is not as popular as **Mother's Day**, the idea is the same; to **honor** and **remember** our fathers and grandfathers. In July we **celebrate Independence Day**, also known as **July 4th**. This is the day we **celebrate** our independence from England so many years ago. We **celebrate** with **fireworks** and **picnics** with **family** and **friends**. September brings **Labor Day**, the official end of summer. It was originally declared as a day to recognize the achievements of American workers in our economic successes. In October, we celebrate **Halloween**. Children dress up in their favorite costumes and go trick-or-treating for candy; many adults participate in the fun and have dress-up **parties**. In November, we celebrate **Thanksgiving Day**. It is a day to remember the early settlers to the new world and their achievements. We gather with **family** and **friends** to **feast** on turkey and other comfort-type foods. In December, we **celebrate Christmas Day**. **Christmas** is a Christian **holiday** that **celebrates** the birth of Jesus Christ. It is also **celebrated** by non-Christians and has many secular-type **celebrations** and **traditions**. Santa Claus visits young children on **Christmas Eve**, leaving toys and games in their stocking. **Hanukkah** is another **holiday celebrated** in December by the Jewish community; an eight-day **holiday commemorating** the rededication of the Holy Temple in Jerusalem. This is only a handful of the **holidays celebrated** by Americans. With so many **holidays**, Americans always have a reason to celebrate; so get out the **decorations**, **balloons**, and **games** and let the **festivities** begin!

Много култури и произходи са представени в Америка. С такова разнообразие американците **празнуват** много **празници** през годината. Има толкова много **празници** в **календара**, винаги има нещо за **празнуване**. През януари **Нова година** е голям **празник**, но истинското празнуване е предишната нощ; има **фойерверки** и **партита**, които се разпространяват по целия свят. През февруари празнуваме **Свети Валентин**. Това е денят, в който повечето двойки изразяват любовта си един към друг с картички и подаръци, През март празнуваме **Деня на Свети Патрик**. Много хора носят зелени неща и празнуват ирландското наследство. **Великден** обикновено се празнува през април. Това е християнски **празник**, но се е превърнал в светски **празник**, който отбелязва началото на пролетта. Един от най-ценените **празници** в Америка е **Денят на майката**. Ние почитаме и си спомняме за нашите майки и баби на този ден, като ги заливаме с картички, подаръци и любов. Друг голям **празник** през май е **Денят на загиналите във войните**;

той първоначално цели да си спомним падналите си **герои** от различни части на армията на Съединените щати. Сега на него се гледа като на неофициално начало на лятото и се празнува с **пикници** и време със **семейството**. През юни ние **празнуваме Деня на бащата**, като той не е толкова популярен като **Деня на майката**, но идеята е същата – да **почетем** и да **си спомним** нашите бащи и дядовци. През юли **празнуваме Деня на независимостта**, който е познат и като **4 юли**. Това е денят, в който **празнуваме** нашата независимост от Англия преди толкова много години. Ние **празнуваме** с **фойерверки** и **пикници** със **семейството** и **приятелите**. Септември носи **Деня на труда**, официалния край на лятото. Той официално е обявен за ден за почитане на постиженията на американските работници в нашия икономически успех. През октомври празнуваме **Хелоуин**. Децата се обличат в любимите си костюми и обикалят за бонбони. Много възрастни участват в забавлението и си правят **партита** с костюми. През ноември празнуваме **Деня на благодарността**. Това е денят, в който си спомняме ранните заселници в новия свят и техните постижения. Събираме се със **семейство** и **приятели**, за да **празнуваме** с пуйка и други храни. През декември **празнуваме Коледа. Коледа** е християнски **празник**, който **празнува** раждането на Исус Христос. Той се **празнува** и от нехристияни и има много светски **празненства** и **традиции**. Дядо Коледа посещава малките деца на **Бъдни вечер**, като оставя играчки и игри в техния чорап. **Ханука** е друг **празник, празнуван** през декември от еврейската общност – осемдневен **празник, отбелязващ** повторното освещаване на Светия храм в Йерусалим. Това е само една малка част от **празниците, празнувани** от американците.

С толкова много **празници**, американците винаги имат причина да празнуват, така че извадете **украсите, балоните** и **игрите** и нека **празниците** започнат!

14) Traveling

airport
летище
le`tisht

backpack
раница
`ranitz

baggage
багаж
bə`gaz

boarding pass
бордна карта
`bordnə `kart

business class
бизнес класа
`biznes `klas

bus station
автобусна спирка
avto`busnə `spirk

carry-on
ръчен
`rəche

check-in

чекиране

che`kirən

coach

автобус

avto`bu

cruise

круиз

kru`i

depart/departure

заминавам/заминаване

zami`navəm/zami`navən

destination

дестинация

desti`natziy

excursion

екскурзия

eks`kurziy

explore

изследвам

iz`sledvə

first class

първа класа

`pʌrvə `klas

flight

полет

`pole

---

flight attendant

стюард(еса)

`styuard/styuar`des

---

fly

летя

le`ty

---

guide

гайд

gay

---

highway

магистрала

məgis`tral

---

hotel

хотел

ho`te

---

inn

хан

ha

---

journey

пътуване

pə`tuvən

---

land

приземявам се

prize`myavəm s

---

landing

кацане

`katzən

---

lift-off

излитане

iz`litən

---

luggage

багаж

bə`gaz

---

map

карта

`kart

---

move

движа се

`dvizhə s

---

motel

мотел

mo`te

---

passenger

пътник

`pʌtni

---

passport
паспорт
pəs`por

pilot
пилот
pi`lo

port
пристанище
pri`stanisht

postcard
картичка
`kartichk

rail
релса
`rels

railway
железопътна линия
zhelezo`pətna `liniy

red-eye
нощен полет
`noshten `pole

reservations
резервации
rezer`vatzi

resort

курорт

ku`ror

---

return

връщане

`vrʌshtən

---

road

път

pʌ

---

roam

скитам

`skitə

---

room

стая

`stay

---

route

маршрут

mərsh`ru

---

safari

сафари

sə`far

---

sail

плавам

`plavə

---

seat

място

`myast

---

sightseeing

разглеждане на забележителности

rəz`glezhdəne na zabele`zhitelnost

---

souvenir

сувенир

suve`ni

---

step

стъпка

`stʌpk

---

suitcase

куфар

`kufə

---

take off

излитам

iz`litə

---

tour

обиколка

obi`kolk

---

tourism

туризъм

tu`rizə

---

tourist

турист

tuˋris

---

traffic

трафик

ˋtrafi

---

trek

дълго и мъчително пътуване

ˋdʌlgo i məˋchitelno pəˋtuvən

---

travel

пътувам

pəˋtuvə

---

travel agent

туристически агент

turisˋticheski əˋgen

---

trip

екскурзия

eksˋkurziy

---

vacation

почивка

poˋchivk

---

voyage

пътуване

pəˋtuvən

Modes of Transportation

airplane/plane

самолет

səmo`le

---

automobile

автомобил

əvtomo`bi

---

balloon

балон

bə`lo

---

bicycle

велосипед

velosi`pe

---

boat

лодка

`lotk

---

bus

автобус

əfto`bu

---

canoe

кану

kə`n

---

car

кола

ko`l

---

ferry

ферибот

`feribo

---

motorcycle

мотоциклет

mototzik`le

---

motor home

кемпер

`kempe

---

ship

кораб

`korə

---

subway

метро

met`r

---

taxi

такси

tak`s

---

train

влак

vla

---

van
микробус
mikro`bu

Hotels

accessible
достъпен
dos`təpe

airport shuttle
автобус до летището
əvto`bus do le`tishtet

all-inclusive
ол инклузив
ol in`kluziv

amenities
удобства
u`dobstv

balcony
балкон
bəl`ko

bathroom
баня
`bany

beach

плаж

plaz

beds

легла

leg`l

bed and breakfast

нощувка със закуска

nosh`tuvkə səs zə`kusk

bellboy/bellhop

пиколо

`pikol

bill

сметка

`smetk

breakfast

закуска

zə`kusk

business center

бизнес център

`bzines `tzentə

cable/satellite tv

кабелна/сателитна телевизия

`kablenə/səte`litnə tele`viziy

charges (in-room)
такси (в хотелска стая)
`taks

check-in
чекиране
che`kirən

check-out
напускане
nə`puskən

concierge
портиер
porti`e

Continental breakfast
европейска закуска
evro`peyskə zə`kusk

corridors (interior)
коридори
kori`dor

doorman
портиер
porti`e

double bed
двойно легло
`dvoyno leg`l

double room

двойна стая

`dvoyna `stay

---

elevator

асансьор

əsən`syo

---

exercise/fitness room

фитнес зала

`fitnes `zal

---

extra bed

допълнително легло

dopəl`nitelno leg`l

---

floor

под

po

---

front desk

рецепция

re`tzeptziy

---

full breakfast

пълна закуска

`pʌlnə zə`kusk

---

gift shop

магазин за подаръци

məgə`zin za po`darətz

guest

гост

gos

---

guest laundry

пране за гости

prə`ne za `gost

---

hair dryer

сешоар

sesho`a

---

high-rise

на много етажи

na mno`go e`tazh

---

hotel

хотел

ho`te

---

housekeeping

домакинство

domə`kinstv

---

information desk

информация

inform`matziy

---

inn

хан

ha

---

in-room
в стаята
v `stayat

internet
интернет
`interne

iron/ironing board
ютия/дъска за гладене
yu`tiya/dəs`ka za `gladen

key
ключ
klyuc

king bed
спалня
`spalny

lobby
лоби
`lob

local calls
местни обаждания
`mestni o`bazhdəniy

lounge
фоайе
foə`y

luggage
багаж
bə`gaz

luxury
луксозен
luk`soze

maid
камериерка
kəmeri`erk

manager
мениджър
`menidzhə

massage
съобщение
səob`shteni

meeting room
конферентна зала
konferen`tna `zal

microwave
микровълнова
mikro`vəlnov

mini-bar
мини бар
`mini ba

motel

мотел

mo`te

---

newspaper

вестник

`vestni

---

newsstand

будка за вестници

`budkə zə `vestnitz

---

non-smoking

за непушачи

za nepu`shach

---

pets/no pets

домашни любимци/без домашни любимци

do`mashni lyu`bimtzi/ bez do`mashni lyu`bimtz

---

pool - indoor/outdoor

басейн – вътрешен/външен

bə`seyn - `vʌnshen/`vʌtreshe

---

porter

портиер

porti`e

---

queen bed

легло персон и половина

leg`lo per`son I polo`vin

---

parking

паркинг

`parkin

---

receipt

касова бележка

`kasovə be`lezhk

---

reception desk

рецепция

re`tzeptziy

---

refrigerator (in-room)

хладилник (в стаята)

hlə`dilnik (v `stayatə

---

reservation

резервация

rezer`vatziy

---

restaurant

ресторант

resto`ran

---

room

стая

`stay

---

room number

номер на стая

`nomer nə `stay

---

room service

рум сървис

rum `sərvi

---

safe (in-room)

сейф

sey

---

service charge

такса за обслужване

`taksə za obs`luzhvən

---

shower

душ

dus

---

single room

единична стая

edi`nichnə `stay

---

suite

апартамент

əpərtə`men

---

tax

данък

`danə

---

tip

бакшиш

bək`shis

---

twin bed

единично легло

edi`nichno leg`l

---

vacancy/ no vacancy

свободни места/няма свободни места

svo`bodni mes`ta/ `nyamə svo`bodni mes`t

---

wake-up call

събуждане по телефона

sə`buzhdəne po tele`fon

---

whirlpool/hot tub

джакузи / хидромасажна вана

dzhə`kuzi / hidromə`sazhnə `van

---

wireless high-speed internet

безжичен високоскоростен интернет

bez`zhichen visoko`skorosten `interne

Related Verbs

to arrive

пристигам

pri`stigə

---

to ask

питам

`pitə

---

to buy

купувам

ku`puvə

to catch a flight

хващам полет

`hvashtəm `pole

to change

прекачвам се

pre`kachvəm s

to drive

карам

`karə

to find

намирам

nə`mirə

to fly

летя

le`ty

to land

кацам

`katzə

to make a reservation

правя резервация

`pravyə rezer`vatziy

to pack

опаковам

opə`kovə

---

to pay

плащам

`plashtə

---

to recommend

препоръчвам

prepo`rəchvə

---

to rent

наемам

na`emə

---

to see

виждам

`vizhdə

---

to stay

отсядам

ot`syadə

---

to take off

излитам

iz`litə

---

to travel

пътувам

pə`tuvə

---

to swim

плувам

`pluvə

Michael is young and adventurous and loves to **travel**; ever since he was a little boy, he has enjoyed the excitement of **traveling**. Whether he **travels** by **boat**, **car**, or **plane**; he always has a great time. Michael has **traveled** all over the world on **vacation**. Once, he took a **bus** from Florida to California, just to say he had done so. His wife enjoys **traveling** with Michael; however, she is not an adventurous person. She likes to **vacation** in nice, quiet places. She prefers an easy **trip** that does not require **layovers** or complicated **itineraries**. Her favorite **destination** is Hawaii, so Michael decided to take her there for their anniversary. They made their **reservations** and took a **plane** from California to Hawaii; or so they thought. That is where this **journey** begins. They bought **tickets** on the **red-eye flight** to get an early start on **vacation**. They arrived at the **airport**, got their **luggage checked-in** and with their **carry-on bags** in hand, they headed towards the **concourse**, ready to **fly** away into the sunset! They were in such a hurry to get to their **destination**; they unknowingly **boarded** the wrong **plane**. They both slept during the **flight** and when they arrived, they both felt something was not quite right; they had traveled to **Alaska**! They checked with their **travel agency** and found out there were no **flights** leaving that **airport** until the next morning. Determined to get to their **vacation** in Hawaii, the couple decided to do whatever it took to get there! They took a **ferry** to the nearest **car** rental location and decided to **drive** as much of the way as possible; they would figure the rest out later. They picked up a **map** and headed on their way. They figured they would get to do some **sightseeing** along the way, if nothing else. It was a long **drive**; they drove for hundreds of miles until they just couldn't drive anymore, so they stopped at a **hotel** to get some rest. The next morning, they **checked-out** of their **hotel room** and continued driving. Their **travel agent** called them and said that they had **coach tickets** the next morning, leaving out of LAX **airport**; they just had to be there in time. The couple made it to the **airport** with just ten minutes to spare! They finally **boarded** their **flight**, on their way to Hawaii. When they arrived at the **airport**, they were so relieved to finally be on **vacation**! They took a **shuttle** to the **resort** and finally were able to enjoy a nice, relaxing **vacation**. Of all Michael's **travels**, this was the most adventurous one yet!

Майкъл е млад и склонен към приключения и обича да **пътува**. Откакто беше малко момче, той се наслаждаваше на вълнението от **пътуването**. Независимо дали **пътува** с **лодка**, **кола** или **самолет**, той винаги си прекарва страхотно. Майкъл е **пътувал** по целия свят на **почивка**. Веднъж той взе **автобус** от Флорида до Калифорния, само за да каже, че го е направил. Съпругата му обича да **пътува** с Майкъл, но тя не е човек, склонен към приключения. Тя обича да **почива** на хубави, тихи места. Тя предпочита лесно **пътуване**, което не изисква **престои** или сложни **маршрути**. Любимата ѝ **дестинация** е Хавай, затова Майкъл реши да я заведе там за годишнината им. Те направиха **резервация** и взеха **самолет** от Калифорния до Хавай или поне така си мислеха. Ето къде започва това **пътуване**. Те купиха **билети** за **нощния полет**, за да започне **почивката** им рано. Пристигнаха на **летището**, **чекираха си багажа** и с **ръчния си багаж** в ръка се запътиха към **тълпата**, готови да **излетят** към залеза! Те толкова бързаха да стигнат до своята **дестинация**, че неволно се **качиха** на грешния **самолет**. И двамата спаха по време на **полета** и когато пристигнаха, и двамата почувстваха, че нещо не е съвсем наред. Бяха отпътували за **Аляска**! Те провериха в **туристическата си агенция** и откриха, че няма **полети** от това **летище** до следващата сутрин. Решени да стигнат до **почивката** си в Хавай, двамата решиха да направят всичко, за да стигнат там! Те взеха **ферибот** до най-близкото място за наемане на **коли** и решиха да **карат** през възможно най-голяма част от пътя и щяха да решат какво да правят после. Те взеха **карта** и тръгнаха. Решиха, че ще **разглеждат забележителности** по пътя, ако не друго. Беше дълъг **път** – пътуваха хиляди мили, докато не можеха да карат вече, затова спряха в **хотел**, за да си починат. На следващата сутрин те **напуснаха хотелската си стая** и продължиха да карат. **Туристическият им агент** им се обади и им каза, че имат **билети** следващата сутрин от **летище** LAX, те просто трябваше да са там навреме. Двойката успя да стигне до **летището,** като имаха само десет минути време! Накрая се **качиха** на **полета** си за Хавай. Когато пристигнаха на **летището**, толкова им олекна, че накрая са на **почивка**! Те взеха **автобус** до **курорта** и накрая можеха да се насладят на хубава, отпускаща **почивка**. От всички **пътувания** на Майкъл това беше най-изпълнето с приключения!

16) School

arithmetic
аритметика
əri`tmetik

assignment
домашна работа
do`mashnə `rabot

atlas
атлас
ət`la

backpack
раница
`ranits

binder
папка
`papk

blackboard
черна дъска
`chernə dəs`k

book
книга
`knig

bookbag

раница

`ranits`

bookcase

библиотека

biblio`tek

bookmark

показалец

pokə`zalet

calculator

калкулатор

kəlku`lato

calendar

календар

kəlen`da

chalk

тебешир

tebe`shi

chalkboard

черна дъска

`chernə dəs`k

chart

диаграма

diəg`ram

class clown

клоунът на класа

klou`nət na klə`s

classmate

съученик

səuche`ni

classroom

класна стая

`klasnə `stay

clipboard

клипборд

`klipbor

coach

треньор

tre`nyo

colored pencils

цветни моливи

`cvetni mo`liv

compass

компас

kom`pa

composition book

тетрадка

tet`radk

computer

компютър

kom`pyutə

construction paper

цветна хартия

`tzvetnə hər`tiy

crayons

пастели

pəs`tel

desk

чин

chi

dictionary

речник

`rechni

diploma

диплома

`dimplom

dividers

делители

de`litel

dormitory

общежитие

obshte`zhiti

dry-erase board
бяла дъска
`byalə dəs`k

easel
статив
stə`ti

encyclopedia
енциклопедия
entziklo`pediy

English
английски
ang`liysk

eraser
гумичка
`gumichk

exam
изпит
`izpi

experiment
експеримент
eksperi`men

flash cards
флаш карти
flash `kart

folder

папка

`papk

---

geography

география

geo`grafiy

---

globe

глобус

`globu

---

glossary

речник на термини

`rechnik na `termin

---

glue

лепило

le`pil

---

gluestick

твърдо лепило

`tvərdo le`pil

---

grades, A, B, C, D, F, passing, failing

оценки, 6,5,4,3,2, минава, не минава

o`tzenki 6,5,4,3,2,, mi`navə, ne mi`nav

---

gym

физкултурен салон

`fizkulturen sə`lo

---

headmaster
директор
di`rekto

---

highlighter
маркер
`marke

---

history
история
is`toriy

---

homework
домашна работа
do`mashnə `rabot

---

ink
мастило
məs`til

---

janitor
портиер
por`tie

Kindergarten
предучилищна
`preduchilishtn

---

keyboard
клавиатура
klaviə`tur

---

laptop

лаптоп

`lapto

lesson

урок

u`ro

library

библиотека

biblio`tek

librarian

библиотекар

bibliote`ka

lockers

шкафчета

`shkafchet

lunch

обяд

o`bya

lunch box/bag

кутия/пакет за обяд

ku`tiya/pə`ket za o`bya

map

карта

`kart

markers
маркери
`marker

math
математика
məte`matik

notebook
тетрадка
tet`ratk

notepad
тефтерче
tef`terch

office
офис
ofi

paper
хартия
hər`tiy

paste
лепило
le`pil

pen
химикал
himi`ka

pencil

молив

mo`li

---

pencil case

кутия за моливи

ku`tiya za mo`liv

---

pencil sharpener

острилка

ost`rilk

---

physical education/PE

физическо възпитание

fi`zichesko vəzpi`tani

---

portfolio

портфолио

`portfoli

---

poster

плакат

plə`ka

---

principal

директор

di`rekto

---

professor

учител

u`chite

---

project
проект
pro`ek

---

protractor
транспортир
transpor`ti

---

pupil
ученик
uche`ni

---

question
въпрос
vəp`ro

---

quiz
викторина
vikto`rin

---

read
чета
che`t

---

reading
четене
`cheten

---

recess
междучасие
mezhdu`chasi

---

ruler

линия

`liniy`

science

наука

`na`uk`

scissors

ножици

`nozhitz`

secretary

секретарка

`sekre`tark`

semester

семестър

`se`mestə`

stapler

телбод

`telbo`

student

ученик

`uche`ni`

tape

тиксо

`tiks`

teacher

учител

u`chite

test

тест

tes

thesaurus

синонимен речник

sino`nimen `rechni

vocabulary

речников запас

`rechnikov zə`pa

watercolors

водни бои

`vodni bo`

whiteboard

бяла дъска

`byalə dəs`k

write

пиша

`pish

Related Verbs

to answer

отговарям

otgoˋvaryə

---

to ask

питам

ˋpitə

---

to draw

рисувам

riˋsuvə

---

to drop out

изключват ме

izˋklyuchvət m

---

to erase

трия

ˋtriy

---

to fail

не минавам

ne miˋnavə

---

to learn

уча

ˋuch

---

to pass

минавам

mi`navə

---

to play

играя

ig`ray

---

to read

чета

che`t

---

to register

записвам се

zə`pisvəm s

---

to show up

появявам се

poya`vyavəm s

---

to sign up

записвам се

zə`pisvəm s

---

to study

уча

`uch

---

to teach

преподавам

prepo`davə

---

to test

тествам

`tetsvə

---

to think

мисля

`misly

---

to write

пиша

`pish

Heather is five years old and has always enjoyed being home with her mom every day. She heard that she would be starting **school** soon and was nervous about it. Summer was coming to an end and Heather was really starting to get anxious about the start of the **school** year. This will be her first and she is unsure about what to expect. She was excited, yet nervous to leave her mom all day. Her mom took her **school supply** shopping on the Saturday before school was to start. She had her list of **school supplies** and was very overwhelmed by all the things in the store. There are so many things on the list, she doesn't know where to start; **crayons**, **paper**, **markers**, **glue**, and more! Heather's mom told her she would need something to put all this stuff in, so she picked out a nice **backpack** with her favorite cartoon cat on it; it also had a matching **lunch bag**! Her mom told her she would also need to get some new clothes because every little girl needs new clothes for the first day of **school**. On the way home from shopping, Heather questioned her mom about **school;** she was getting very excited because she wondered what she would be doing with all this stuff! The first day of **school** finally came and Heather's mom took her to register for the first day of **Kindergarten**. The first stop was the **office**, she met a very nice lady, the **school secretary**, and she also met a handsome gentleman who said he was the **principal** of the **school**. She wasn't sure what that meant, but he must be important. Once everything was settled in the **office**, her mom took her to her new **classroom**. When she walked in, she couldn't believe her eyes; it was amazing! There was a big **chalkboard** on the wall, rows of **desks**, colorful **charts** and **maps**, even some games and **books**. She really likes games and **books**, so she started to relax a bit. Then, she saw her new **teacher**; she was a nice lady, smiling and being very polite. Heather then realized she would be okay. She sent her mom on her way and told her she would see her this afternoon after **school.** She was ready to learn to **read** and **write**, do **math** and **science**; she was not nervous anymore! That day she made several new friends and really like her **teacher**. They had **English** and **Math**; she even got to paint using her new **watercolors**. Heather decided she loved **school** and wanted to come back every day!

Хедър е на пет и винаги е обичала да стои вкъщи с майка си всеки ден. Тя научи, че ще започва **училище** скоро и беше неспокойна заради това. Лятото свършваше и Хедър наистина започваше да се тревожи за началото на **учебната** година. Тя ще ѝ бъде първа и Хедър не знаеше какво да очаква. Майка ѝ я заведе на пазар за **училищни пособия** в събота преди началото на училището. Тя имаше първия си списък с **училищни пособия** и беше много объркана от всичките неща в магазина. Има толкова много неща в списъка ѝ, че не знае откъде да започне: **пастели, хартия, маркери, лепило** и други! Майката на Хедър ѝ каза, че ще ѝ трябва нещо, в което да сложи всичките тези неща, затова тя си избра красива **раница** с любимата й анимационна котка на нея. Имаше и същата **торба за обяд**! Майка й и каза, че ще й трябват и нови дрехи, защото всяко малко момиче се нуждае от нови дрехи за първия си ден в **училище**. По пътя към вкъщи Хедър разпитваше майка си за **училището**. Тя много се вълнуваше, защото се чудеше какво ще прави с всички тези неща! Първият **учебен** ден най-накрая дойде и майката на Хедър я заведе да се запише за първия ден на **предучилищна**. Първата спирка беше **офисът**; тя срещна много любезна дама – **училищната секретарка** и красив джентълмен, който каза, че е **директорът** на **училището**. Тя не беше сигурна какво означава това, но той изглежда беше важен. След като всичко беше уредено в **офиса**, майка й я заведе до новата й **класна стая**. Когато влезе, не можеше да повярва на очите си – беше невероятна! Имаше голяма **черна дъска** на стената, редици с **чинове**, цветни **диаграми** и **карти**, дори някои игри и **книги**. Тя наистина обича игри и **книги**, затова започна да се отпуска малко. След това видя новата си **учителка** – тя беше приятна дама, усмихната и много любезна. Тогава Хедър разбра, че ще се справи. Тя изпрати майка си и й каза, че ще се видят следобеда след **училище**. Тя беше готова да се научи да **чете** и **пише,** да учи **математика** и **наука**. Вече не беше разтревожена! Този ден тя се сприятели с няколко нови човека и наистина харесваше **учителката** си. Имаха **английски** и **математика**. Дори трябваше да рисува с новите си **водни бои**. Хедър реши, че обича **училището** и искаше да се връща там всеки ден!

17) Hospital

ache
болка
`bolk

---

acute
остър
`ostə

---

allergy/allergic
алергия/алергичен
ə`lergiya//əler`giche

---

ambulance
линейка
li`neyk

---

amnesia
амнезия
əm`neziy

---

amputation
ампутация
əmpu`taciy

---

anaemia
анемия
ə`nemiy

---

anesthesiologist

анестезиолог

ənestezio`lo

antibiotics

антибиотици

ənti`biotitz

anti-depressant

антидепресанти

`antidepre`sant

appointment

уговорен час

ugo`voren cha

arthritis

артрит

ərt`ri

asthma

астма

`astm

bacteria

бактерия

bək`teriy

bedsore

рана от пролежаване

`ranə ot prole`zhavən

biopsy

биопсия

biop`siy

---

blood

кръв

krʌ

---

blood count

кръвна картина

`krʌvna kər`tin

---

blood donor

донор на кръв

`donor na krʌ

---

blood pressure

кръвно налягане

`krʌvno nə`lyagən

---

blood test

кръвни изследвания

`krʌvni iz`sledvəniy

---

bone

кост

kos

---

brace

протектор

pro`tekto

---

bruise

натъртване

nə`tʌrtvən

Caesarean section (C-section)

Цезарово сечение

`tzezərovo se`cheni

---

cancer

рак

ra

---

cardiopulmonary resuscitation (CPR)

кардиопулмонална реанимация (КПР)

`kardiopulmo`nalnə reəni`maciya

---

case

случай

`slucha

---

cast

гипсова превръзка

`gipsovə prev`rʌzk

---

chemotherapy

химиотерапия

`himiote`rapiy

---

coroner

съдебен лекар

sə`deben `lekə

---

critical

критичен

kri`tiche

---

crutches

патерици

`pateritz

---

cyst

киста

`kist

---

deficiency

недостатъчност

nedo`statəchnos

---

dehydrated

дехидратиран

`dehidrə`tira

---

diabetes

диабет

diə`be

---

diagnosis

диагноза

diəg`noz

---

dietician

диетолог

dieto`lo

---

disease

болест

`boles

---

doctor

лекар

`lekə

---

emergency

спешен случай

`speshen `sluchə

---

emergency room (ER)

спешно отделение

`speshno otde`leni

---

exam

преглед

`pregle

---

fever

треска

`tresk

---

flu (influenza)

грип

gri

---

fracture

фрактура

frək`tur

---

heart attack
сърдечен удар
sər`dechen `udə

hematologist
хематолог
hemәto`lo

hives
уртикария
urti`kariy

hospital
болница
`bolnitz

illness
болест
`boles

imaging
образна диагностика
`obrәznә diәg`nostik

immunization
имунизация
imuni`zaciy

infection
инфекция
in`fekciy

Intensive Care Unit (ICU)

реанимация

reəni`maciy

IV

интравенозен

`intrəve`noze

laboratory (lab)

лаборатория

ləborə`toriy

life support

поддържане на живота

pod`dərzəne na zhi`vot

mass

маса

`mas

medical technician

медицински техник

medi`tzinski teh`ni

neurosurgeon

неврохирург

`nevrohi`rur

nurse

медицинска сестра

medi`tzinskə ses`tr

operating room (OR)
операционна
operə`tzionnə

operation
операция
ope`ratziy

ophthalmologist
офталмолог
oftəmo`lo

orthopedic
ортопедичен
ortope`diche

pain
болка
`bolk

patient
пациент
pətzi`en

pediatrician
педиатър
pedi`atə

pharmacist
фармацевт
fərmə`tzev

pharmacy

аптека

əp`tek

physical Therapist

физиотерапевт

`fizioterə`pev

physician

лекар

`lekə

poison

отрова

ot`rov

prescription

рецепта

re`tzept

psychiatrist

психиатър

psihi`atə

radiologist

рентгенолог

rentgeno`lo

resident

стажант

stə`zhan

scan

преглед на скенер

`pregled na `skene

scrubs

хирургическа престилка

hirur`gicheskə pres`tilk

shots

подкожни инжекции

pod`kozhni in`zhektzi

side effects

странични ефекти

strə`nichni e`fekt

specialist

специалист

spetziə`lis

stable

стабилен

stə`bile

surgeon

хирург

hi`rur

symptoms

симптоми

simp`tom

therapy

терапия

te`rapiy

---

treatment

лечение

le`cheni

---

vein

вена

`ven

---

visiting hours

часове за посещение

chəso`ve za pose`shteni

---

visitor

посетител

pose`tite

---

wheelchair

инвалидна количка

invə`lidnə ko`lichk

---

x-ray

рентген

`rentge

Related Verbs

to bring

нося

`nosy

---

to cough

кашлям

`kashlya

---

to examine

преглеждам

preg`lezhdə

---

to explain

обяснявам

obyas`nyavə

---

to feel

чувствам

`chuvstvə

---

to give

давам

`davəm

---

to hurt

наранявам

nərə`nyavə

---

to prescribe

предписвам

pred`pisvə

to scan

преглеждам на скенер

preg`lezhdəm na `skene

to take

взимам

`vzimə

to test

изследвам

iz`sledvə

to treat

лекувам

le`kuvəm

to visit

посещавам

pose`shtavə

to wait

чакам

`chakə

to x-ray

гледам на рентген

`gledəm na `rentge

James was a happy, **healthy** ten year old boy who loved sports and riding his bike; but one day that all came to a halt. James had been complaining that his back was hurting. The **pain** was so bad one morning; he couldn't even get out of bed. His mom decided to take him to the **emergency room** to get **examined** by a **doctor**. The **nurses** were very friendly and their number one priority was making sure James was not in **pain** and could rest comfortably. The **doctor** decided to order an **x-ray** of his back. The **radiologist** read the report; he and the **ER doctor** agreed that James had an unknown **mass** on his spine. James was immediately admitted to the **hospital** for **blood tests**. The **blood tests** did not reveal the cause of the **mass,** so the **pediatrician** overseeing his **case** decided he needed some more extensive **imaging tests**, as well as a **biopsy**. James was nervous because so many **doctors** were coming to see him; an **orthopedic doctor**, a **neurosurgeon,** and a **hematologist.** The **nurses** did a good job at keeping his mind at ease. They brought him movies and video games to play to keep him busy. He had many **visitors**; friends and family members came to see him. He loved the visits with the **therapy** dogs the most; they were such comforting and sweet dogs. They had so many activities and fun for the **patients** at the children's **hospital**. James was a real trooper when they had to take **blood** and put his **IV** in his arm. James spent twelve days in the **hospital** before they finally **diagnosed** him with a **bone infection**. The **physical therapist** fit him with a back brace and he was **prescribed antibiotics**. After undergoing multiple **blood tests, image scans**, and a **biopsy**, James was ready to go home. He was not able to do the normal things other kids could do because of the damage to his spine, but he was so happy to be home with his family and on the mend from his terrible back **infection**. After several months of **treatment** and spinal **surgery** to straighten his back, James is now a strong, healthy, and happy boy. Through it all; the t**reatments, tests, hospital** stays, and **therapy**, James has been an inspiration and hero to many who walked this journey with him.

Джеймс беше щастливо, **здраво** десетгодишно момче, което обичаше спортове и да кара своето колело, но един ден всичко това спря. Джеймс се оплакваше, че го боли гърбът. **Болката** беше толкова силна едно сутрин, че той дори не можеше да стане от леглото. Майка му реши да го заведе в **спешното отделение**, за да бъде **прегледан** от **лекар**. **Сестрите** бяха много любезни и техен приоритет беше да се уверят, че Джеймс не го **боли** и може да си почива спокойно. **Лекарят** реши да поръча **рентген** за гърба му. **Рентгенологът** прочете картона.Той и **лекарят от спешното** се съгласиха, че Джеймс има непозната **маса** на гръбнака си. Джеймс беше незабавно приет в **болница** за **кръвни изследвания**. **Кръвните изследвания** не разкриха причината за **масата**, затова **педиатърът**, наблюдаващ неговия случай, реши, че той се нуждае от по-разширени **образни изследвания**, както и **биопсия**. Джеймс беше разтревожен, защото толкова много **лекари** идваха да го видят – **ортопед, неврохирург** и **хематолог**. **Сестрите** свършиха страхотна работа, поддържайки го спокоен. Те му донесоха филми и видео игри, които да играе, за да е зает. Той имаше много **посетители** – приятели и членове на семейството идваха да го видят. Той обичаше посещенията с кучета за **терапия** най-много – те бяха толкова успокояващи и сладки кучета. Имаше толкова много дейности и забавления за **пациентите** в детската **болница**. Джеймс беше истински герой, когато трябваше да му вземат **кръв** и да му сложат **система** на ръката. Джеймс прекара дванайсет дни в **болницата**, преди накрая да му сложат **диагноза инфекция на костите**. Лекарят му даде **протектор** и му **предписа антибиотик**. След като мина няколко **кръвни теста, снимки** и **биопсия**, Джеймс беше готов да се прибере вкъщи. Той не можеше да прави нормалните неща, които другите деца можеха да правят, заради увреждането на гръбнака му, но той беше толкова щастлив да си бъде вкъщи със семейството си и на път да оздравее от тази ужасна **инфекция** на гърба. След няколко месеца на **лечение** и гръбначна **операция** за изправяне на гърба, Джеймс сега е силно, здраво и щастливо момче. През цялото това време – **лечението, изследванията,** престоя в **болницата** и **терапията**, Джеймс беше вдъхновение и герой за много хора, които извървяха пътя с него.

18) Emergency

accident
инцидент
intzi`den

---

aftershock
вторичен трус
vto`richen tru

---

ambulance
линейка
li`neyk

---

asthma attack
астматичен пристъп
əstmə`tichen `pristə

---

avalanche
лавина
lə`vin

---

blizzard
виелица
vi`elitz

---

blood/bleeding
кръв/кървене
krʌv/kər`ven

broken bone

счупена кост

`schupenə kos

car accident

автомобилна катастрофа

əvtomo`bilnə kətəs`trof

chest pain

болка в гърдите

`bolkə v gər`dit

choking

задавяне

zə`davyan

coast guard

брегова охрана

brego`va oh`ran

crash

катастрофа

kətəs`trof

diabetes

диабет

diə`be

doctor

лекар

`lekə

drought

суша

`sush

drowning

удавяне

u`davyən

earthquake

земетресение

zemetre`seni

emergency

спешен случай

`speshen `slucha

emergency services

служби за спешна помощ

`sluzhbi za `speshnə `pomosh

EMT (emergency medical technician)

спешен медицински техник

`speshen medi`tzinski teh`ni

explosion

експлозия

eks`ploziy

fight

битка

`bitk

fire

пожар

po`zha

---

fire department

пожарна

po`zharn

---

fire escape

авариен изход

əvə`rien `izho

---

firefighter

пожарникар

pozhərni`ka

---

fire truck

пожарна кола

po`zharnə ko`l

---

first aid

първа помощ

`pлərvə `pomosh

---

flood

наводнение

nəvod`neni

---

fog

мъгла

məg`l

---

gun
оръжие
o`rʌzhi

---

gunshot
изстрел
`izstre

---

heart attack
сърдечен удар
sər`dechen `udə

---

heimlich maneuver
Хаймлиш маневра
`haymlish mə`nevr

---

help
помощ
`pomosh

---

hospital
болница
`bolnitz

---

hurricane
ураган
urə`ga

---

injury
нараняване
nərə`nyavən

---

ladder

стълба

`stʌlb

---

lifeguard

телохранител

telohrə`nite

---

life support

поддръжка на живота

pod`drʌzhkə na zhi`vot

---

lightening

светкавица

svet`kavitzə

---

lost

изгубен

iz`gube

---

mudslide

кално свлачище

`kalno `svlachisht

---

natural disaster

природно бедствие

pri`rodno `bedstvi

---

nurse

медицинска сестра

medi`tzinskə ses`tr

---

officer
офицер
ofiˋtze

paramedic
парамедик
ˋparəˋmedi

poison
отрова
oˋtrov

police
полиция
poˋlitziy

police car
полицейска кола
poliˋtzeyskə koˋl

rescue
спасяване
spəˋsyavən

robbery
обир
ˋobi

shooting
стрелба
strelˋb

stop

стоп

sto

storm

буря

`bury

stroke

удар

`udə

temperature

температура

temperə`tur

thief

крадец

krə`det

tornado

торнадо

tor`nad

tsunami

цунами

tzu`nam

unconscious

в безсъзнание

v bezsəz`nani

weather emergency

природно бедствие

pri`rodno `bedstvi

Related Verbs

to bleed

кървя

kər`vy

to break

чупя

`chupy

to breathe

дишам

`dishə

to burn

горя

go`ry

to call

обаждам се

o`bazhdəm s

to crash

катастрофирам

kətəstro`firə

to cut

порязвам

po`ryazvə

to escape

бягам

`byagə

to faint

припадам

pri`padə

to fall

падам

`padə

to help

помагам

po`magə

to hurt

наранявам

nərə`nyavə

to rescue

спасявам

spə`syavə

to save

спасявам

spə`syavə

to shoot

стрелям

stre`lya

---

to wheeze

дишам трудно

`dishəm `trudn

---

to wreck

разбивам се

rəz`bivəm se

One of the most important things parents can teach their children is how to handle an **emergency**. You often hear stories on the news about a child who saved someone by making a wise decision in an **emergency**. What you don't hear are the stories when children made a poor decision. Unfortunately, many children would not know what to do in case of a real **emergency** such as a **fire**, a **flood**, or if a parent had a **heart attack**. We hope that our children are never put in these situations, but we want them to be prepared. In an **emergency**, such as a **tornado**, an **earthquake**, or other **natural disaster**, children might react in two very dangerous ways; one of which is the superhero reaction. In this case, children think they can "save the day" and play **rescue** worker. They might try to run into a burning building or swim out to save someone in a **flood**. Make sure your children know that there are people such as **firefighters**, **police officers**, and **EMTs** that are professionally trained to handle these situations. It may seem safe to "**help**", but the danger may not be obvious to a child. If they try to "**help**" in a dangerous situation, it may make the **emergency** worse! The best thing to do is call **emergency services** and they will tell you exactly what you can do to **help**. On the other hand, the opposite reaction can be just as dangerous. Some children will try to run and hide from scary situations. Even though you may be scared, try to remain calm, find a phone, and call for **help**. As I said earlier, children often play a big role in the **rescue** efforts during an **emergency**. Here are some practical tips to teach your children about **emergency** situations. 1) Take a deep breath, relax and look around for **help**. 2) Call for **help**; either by yelling or phone. If someone has an **injury** or are hurt, the **rescue** workers can be there fast. In a **life threatening** situation, the **emergency operator** can often walk you through step-by-step what to do. 3) Never hang up on the operator; they will need details about your location and the **emergency** situation. 4) Find a safe place to wait for help. Do not put yourself in danger while you wait for the professionals, it will only create a bigger **emergency**. The best way to handle an **emergency** is to prepare yourself for one. If you know what to do in different **emergencies**, you will be better equipped to handle them. Ask your parents to teach you the **fire escape** plan in your home or what to do in case someone is **injured** at home. Ask someone to show you how to call for help; make sure the phone numbers for the **fire department**, **police**, and **ambulance** service numbers are posted on your home phone. As you get older, you can even take a **first aid** class. Remember, in all **emergencies**, remain calm and call for help and never put yourself in danger.

Едно от най-важните неща, на които родителите могат да научат децата си, е как да се справят при **спешен случай**. Често чувате истории по новините за това как дете спасява някого, като взима мъдро решение при

спешен случай. Това, за което не чувате, са историите как децата взимат грешно решение. За жалост, много деца не биха знаели какво трябва да направят при истински **спешен случай**, като **пожар, наводнение** или ако родителят получи **сърдечен удар**. Надяваме се, че нашите деца никога не биха попаднали в такива ситуации, но искаме те да бъдат подготвени. При **спешен случай**, като **торнадо, земетресение** или друго **природно бедствие**, децата могат да реагират по два много опасни начина, единият от които е реакцията на супергерой. В този случай децата си мислят, че могат да „спасят положението" и си играят на **спасителен** работник. Те може да опитат да влязат в горяща сграда или да плуват, за да спасят някого в **наводнение**. Уверете се, че децата ви знаят, че има хора, като **пожарникари, полицаи** и **спешни медицински техници**, които са професионално обучени да се справят с тези ситуации. Може да изглежда безопасно да „**помогнеш**", но опасността може да не е видима за едно дете. Ако то се опита да „**помогне**" в опасна ситуация, това може да направи **спешния случай** по-лош! Най-доброто, което може да направи, е да се обади на **службите за спешна помощ** и те ще кажат точно какво можете да направи, за да помогне. От друга страна, другата реакция може да бъде също толкова опасна. Някои деца ще се опитат да избягат и да се скрият от страшна ситуация. Дори и да сте уплашени, опитайте се да останете спокойни, намерете телефон и се обадете за **помощ**. Както казах по-рано, децата често играят голяма роля в усилията за **спасяване** при **спешен случай**. Ето няколко практически съвета, които да дадете на своите деца за **спешните случаи**: 1) Поемете си въздух, успокойте се и потърсете **помощ**. 2) Потърсете **помощ**, викайки или по телефона. Ако някой е **ранен, спасителните** работници може да пристигнат бързо. В **животозастрашаваща** ситуация **операторът** може да ви упъти какво да направите стъпка по стъпка. 3) Никога не затваряйте на оператора – той ще се нуждае от подробности за вашето местоположение при **спешен случай**. 4) Намерете безопасно място и изчакайте помощ. Не се излагайте на опасност, докато чакате професионалистите – това само ще създаде още по-неприятна **ситуация**. Най-добрият начин да се справите със **спешен случай** е да се подготвите за такъв. Ако знаете какво да правите в различни **спешни случаи**, ще бъдете по-добре подготвени да се справите с тях. Попитайте родителите си да ви покажат плана за **аварийния изход** във вашия дом или какво да направите, ако някой вкъщи е **ранен**. Попитайте някого да ви покаже как да се обадите за помощ. Уверете се, че телефонните номера за **пожарната, полицията** и **спешната помощ** са на домашния ви телефон. Когато пораснете, може да минете и обучение по **първа помощ**. Помнете – във всички **спешни случаи** останете спокойни и се обадете за помощ, а никога не се излагайте на опасност.